Advance Praise for *MAN*ifesting*

"*MAN*ifesting* is filled with inspiration, authenticity, and empowerment, instilling the belief that you will find your 'person.' Jaime Bronstein is beyond insightful, and *MAN*ifesting* is a must-read!"

> —Jen Gottlieb, International Speaker and Co-Founder of Super Connector Media

"*MAN*ifesting* provides an incredible set of tools and exercises to elevate each reader's mindset in their journey to finding love."

> —Ashley Stahl, *Forbes* Columnist and Host of *You Turn* Podcast

"*MAN*ifesting* is packed with profound and insightful teachings for anyone looking for love but having trouble finding it."

> —Stacy Igel, Global Clothing Brand Founder/CCO of BOY MEETS GIRL® and Author of *Embracing the Calm in the Chaos* (Harper Collins)

"As someone who already has a very strong intuition, Jaime taught me to pay attention and TRUST YOUR GUT!!!! You'll thank yourself later, promise."

> —Kenley Stevenson, Editor, HGTV Magazine

"*MAN*ifesting* offers Jaime Bronstein's hard-won wisdom, along with step-by-step guidance that will be the catalyst to create the love life of your dreams."

—Arielle Ford, Author of *The Soulmate Secret*

"Single or not, this book is a must-read for a successful and healthy relationship! Jaime teaches readers how to push those doubts aside and 'reclaim your authentic self.' Even when the dating scene gets tough, this book will remind you to keep your standards high, don't settle, and manifest what you want. This is the last relationship book you'll ever need. The teachings in *MAN*ifesting* are profound and life-changing!"

—Taylor Knight, Emmy Award–Winning Journalist

"Jaime Bronstein's *MAN*ifesting* is a game changer, especially in this new post-Covid climate where mental health awareness is KEY. This book teaches communication and self-awareness, self-worth, and living our positive, true authentic lives. Jaime's book helps everyone of every age and gender set goals to live a positively changed life. A must-read!"

—Marki Costello, President of the Creative Management Entertainment Group

MAN♥ifesting

A STEP-BY-STEP GUIDE

TO ATTRACTING THE LOVE

THAT IS MEANT FOR YOU

JAIME BRONSTEIN, LCSW

Post Hill
PRESS

A POST HILL PRESS BOOK
ISBN: 978-1-63758-670-9
ISBN (eBook): 978-1-63758-671-6

MAN*ifesting:
A Step-by-Step Guide to Attracting the Love That Is Meant for You
© 2023 by Jaime Bronstein, LCSW
All Rights Reserved

Cover design by Kaitlyn Rodenbucher

Post Hill Press
New York • Nashville
posthillpress.com

Published in the United States of America
1 2 3 4 5 6 7 8 9 10

To my parents, my angels on earth, to Bryan, the man I "MAN*ifested," and to our son, Noah, who we "son*ifested" together. I am beyond grateful for all of your love and support; it means more to me than you'll ever know.

Table of Contents

FOREWORD

WHAT RADIO STATION ARE you listening to? When it comes to your love life, are you listening to "LonelyandMiserable" FM, where all the songs are negative, or are you listening to the "I'm Happy, Loved, and Content" channel?

We all have the power, in every moment, to select the frequency we wish to vibrate and manifest at. And just like the law of gravity is always working, whether we are aware of it or not, the power of manifestation is always working, drawing to us the people, places, and experiences that match our thoughts and state of being.

Do you ever wonder why so many smart, successful, beautiful women struggle with finding The One? There are a zillion answers to this, but I believe it comes down to a few things: we like to spend our time doing the things we excel at, like working, and we freak out and avoid the stuff we have a problem with, like dating, healing our inner wounds and blocks to love, or doing our taxes.

And, perhaps most importantly, we don't have the playbook on how to use our powers of manifestation for love (or we read a book or took a workshop but never implemented the actual steps to make it happen). I've been studying manifestation for the past thirty-five years and along the way have discovered that not only does it really, really work, it's also very slippery.

You can fully understand it one moment and the next feel muddled and confused. Especially when the results aren't anywhere close to instantaneous.

It's up to each and every one of us to manage our thoughts, feelings, and actions so that we can ultimately manifest The One (and anything else our heart desires). Manifesting is both an art and a science, and there is a recipe that works when you put together all the right ingredients.

Just like you wouldn't buy a cookbook from a novice chef or take investing advice from a person on welfare, I believe you should only take *finding love* advice from a happily married expert who can shine a bright light on the path for you. Jaime Bronstein is such an expert.

This book offers her hard-won wisdom, along with step-by-step guidance that will be the catalyst to create the love life of your dreams.

She has been where you are right now, alone and dreaming of love, and she can guide you to where you want to be if you are willing to invest a little time, energy, and trust into the process.

Along the way, you will discover a new willingness to believe in yourself, to believe in love, and to know that the one you are looking for is also looking for you.

And, of course, we all have days when we doubt and our thoughts go into a dark place, so don't beat yourself up when that happens—just stay aware and remember to change the channel.

Wishing you love, laughter, and magical kisses,

Arielle Ford
Author of *The Soulmate Secret: Manifest the Love of Your Life with the Law of Attraction*

INTRODUCTION

Affirmation: *"I no longer live in the past, and I forgive myself and everyone in my life. I know that everything that has happened, has happened for a reason, and I am ready to heal."*

I SAT DOWN IN my chair and watched Jenna get settled on the couch. This was her third session. Jenna was a young woman approaching twenty-eight. She had reached out to me to work through why she wasn't married yet, having watched all her friends get engaged and married, some even start families. For a while, she was fine with that. Jenna had a great career that she could pour her heart and soul into. But today she was finally at the point where she admitted that she wasn't happy being single.

Jenna was ready to find love.

We'd unpacked her past in her first two sessions, and now it was time to move beyond her history and get into the work of figuring out what was holding her back today. She was ready to change her life.

"So, how was your week?" I asked.

Most of the time I can lead with an open-ended question, and the issue my client is eager to discuss will come out, no matter what question I ask. Jenna began to tell me about going to a bar on Friday night with some friends, in hopes of meeting someone. The night ended in disappointment, as usual. She was tired of the kinds of guys who showed up at bars, anyway.

I nodded.

"Do you use any of the dating apps?" I asked.

She looked at me in horror, as if I'd just asked her if she'd robbed a bank.

"No!" she said, full of defensiveness. "I don't want to use an app. I want to meet my man organically. Like at the farmers' market, or at a party. I can't stand the apps. Plus, do I look like someone who needs apps to find my man? No way!"

I nodded my head again and smiled. I could see what was blocking Jenna from finding love already.

I'm a relationship therapist, and I see the many ways the dating landscape has changed. I absolutely understand not wanting to meet your future husband on an app, but what I was worried about was not Jenna's dislike of dating technology. I was more concerned with her insistence that her love story had to look a certain way.

The Universe doesn't like being dictated to. There is a difference between setting an intention and stipulating a plan. The Universe responds most abundantly to our desires when it senses that we are relaxed, open, and ready for what it has in store.

Most women who walk into my office are not relaxed. Sometimes I can physically see the tension in their body as they settle in on the couch and awkwardly place their hands on their lap. They've likely come to tell me about their fear that they will pick the wrong man *again* because they did in the past. Like you, they didn't know any better. They thought it must be love because of what was on paper but didn't feel peace in their heart, while others had fallen in love previously, knew how it felt, and now they weren't feeling even close to that level for their husband but married him anyway. Other women have come to see me to ask if they will ever find love, or if they will be single forever. There are even women who are hopeful for love after divorce or widows who believe there is love after love. I receive many emails day after day entitled "Contemplating a breakup," illustrating that there are many women who need some guidance to gain their clarity and who could also use some empowerment to trust themselves and their feelings. Every woman is different and every client brings their own beautiful and precious stories to the table, but what they all have in common is that they all want to be happy and in a healthy relationship. They want to be healed and to leave the past in the past. They want to be free from the self-inflicting suffering that they feel daily because they don't have what they want (and many blame themselves; it's their fault that they aren't married yet, which could not be further from the truth). I also want to mention that if you are a man who wants to MAN*ifest, please replace "woman" with "man" and any female pronouns with male pronouns.

THE PURPOSE OF THIS BOOK

My purpose in this book is to help women who are looking for love to first cultivate a stronger connection with themselves, to really *listen* and *trust themselves*.

I want you to get in touch with your intuition to make the best, most informed decisions as you navigate your dating journey to the ultimate decision of whom you will marry. You need to be connected with yourself in order to manifest the right connection with the right man.

No one feels super comfortable the first time they walk into a new therapist's office. Good thing I'm not your white-coat psychotherapist or the psychologist in the leatherback chair. I'm real, and I aim to be relatable. I share tidbits of my own life with clients who come to see me for relationship coaching. I want them to know that my office is a safe space in which to relax, open up, and release the fears that have been shackling them. We are all human, and we all have inner dialogues and fears.

My job is to guide you to wake up and see how you are limiting your own love stories and holding yourself back from finding love. As a longtime student and practitioner of spiritual psychology, I strongly believe that our thoughts get in our way and hold us back from the love that is waiting for us. You see, our outside experiences are reflections of our inner reality, so if we are disconnected from ourself (our authentic self, our soul), feeling bad, and living life believing we are unworthy of love, The Universe will honor exactly that. Through the law of attraction, it will bring us men who validate that we are not worthy of love, because that is what we believe about ourselves. That's the message we are sending. I teach women how to get out of their own way, heal their unresolved issues, connect with themselves, get empowered, and show up in life and love from that place.

The rest is history, or shall I say *her*-story! Sooner rather than later, her man seemingly appears "out of nowhere" just in time to restore her faith in love. You see, he was never very far away. He was just waiting for her to know her worth instead of him telling her what she herself needed to believe. We must love ourselves first. We must know that love, self-love, and the love we receive from The One, is what we deserve. Love is our birthright.

"OK," I said to Jenna, as she looked at me, the disdain over dating apps still lingering on her face. "So, you don't want to meet your man on an app. I get that. You can certainly pretend to be in control of your love story, but by staying in that place of perceived control, you will never be able to move forward. However, by releasing the control and seeing what unfolds, that, my dear, is how to manifest love. Be open to what is, and what could be, and let The Universe bring love into your life."

I'm not sure Jenna liked what I had to say that day, but I could see in her face that a light bulb had turned on. I knew a shift was beginning to happen. She and I talked some more and began to explore the concept of openness and the many paths of love, and before I knew it, I glanced at the clock and realized that it was almost fifty past the hour. Jenna left that day intrigued. When she came back the next week, we began to work through the many ways she could open herself up to love and discussed the many ways love might already be trying to come into her life.

News flash: you might not meet your guy in the perfect way you dreamed of as a little girl. But I can promise you that even though you may not meet him the exact way you planned (online perhaps!), your relationship can still be everything you imagined it would be. And, at the end of the day, isn't it more important that you meet your man, *period*, no matter how it happens?

I remember all too well what it was like to be in Jenna's shoes. I didn't meet my husband until I was thirty-four, and we didn't get married until I was thirty-seven. If you had told me at twenty-two that I wouldn't get married for fifteen years, I would have been devastated. Today, I wouldn't change a thing about what led me to Bryan. Plus, it gave me a lot of years in the trenches and the kind of experiences that help me have empathy and understanding for the women who sit across from me. I've been in their shoes (especially the stilettos that kill our feet and make us stumble!), and today I'm on the other side, fully grounded (wearing comfy shoes) and ready to hold out a helping hand as they wobble their way toward love. I'm committed to helping you bulldoze through all the muck that is keeping you stuck, so you can move forward and start manifesting The One who is just right for you.

It took me time to get these comfy shoes, but I've come to understand that my stiletto years couldn't have gone any other way. There was a lot I needed to learn, connect with, and love within myself. Growing up, I was the "love girl," always coaching my friends through their relationship woes. As an undergrad at Boston University, I majored in psychology (the romantic relationship discussions in class were my favorite). Then two years after college, I went to New York University for graduate school and got a master's degree in social work. While I became my friends' "therapist," (they would ask me my opinion on "Spencer" or "Hunter" over mimosas at Sunday brunches), I overanalyzed the romantic connections I was having with the many men I dated in New York, but never seemed to achieve the relationship I desired. (I had SO much to learn!) After grad school, I went across the country to Los Angeles, where I became a professional relationship therapist and learned how to coach others to find their person. Yet, I didn't understand why it was taking so long for *me* to find my own person because my whole life was dedicated to relationships; I felt I should know better. As I started to watch not only clients but also friends and colleagues find their happily ever after, I struggled with the fact that I was still going on first dates—and I was a successful relationship coach in my thirties! It felt like my happily married friends were all in a club I was born to be a part of, but life wasn't letting me join.

I had to kiss a bunch of frogs and a few pseudo-princes. I rationalized some not-so-wise choices and then had to learn to forgive myself, not only for the rationalizing but also for thinking that *this time* would be different. This time things would change. This time answering the booty call would result in deeper intimacy. *We will bond so much—this time!—when we have a sleepover, because the next morning, over breakfast in bed, me with wild bedhead and him with fresh coffees, we will get to know each other SO much better.* That was the dream, but the reality was quite different. Let's just say that I was no stranger to the walk of shame.

Oh, younger Jaime, you had so much to learn. And that is completely OK. We learn because we are human, and learning is all part of growing to recognize our worth.

You have picked up this book, which means you are ready to do things differently. You are ready to learn. You are ready for this book to *monumentally* change your life.

THE LOVE AND LAW OF ATTRACTION

I know how hard it can be to watch others find their matches, get their fairy-tale weddings, and start having families. It is easy to create a story in your head saying that there is something wrong with you and that it will never happen. Those thoughts, those words, and those stories have power; in this book, I'm going to teach you how to stop those stories in their tracks.

I call this book *MAN*ifesting* because I believe in the law of attraction. Like attracts like. What you put out there, you get back in return. So, when you start to tell the story that *you'll never find The One, that there are no good guys left, that this relationship is sure to end in heartbreak*, guess what happens? Since The Universe gives us what we focus on, it picks up on those signals and delivers exactly what you are asking for—you never finding The One.

To heal, you must change your story. This means change the story upstairs and the one deep in your heart, and then you will change your reality in real life. We are the co-creators of our lives. It is totally normal to have some unhealthy stories, but with the help of this book we're going to clear them out. We're going to remove the negativity and fear, and in their place fill you up with a celebration of who you are, a deep trust in The Universe, and the complete and total conviction that your person is out there and on his way to meet you at the perfect time.

Now, some therapists say that to find love, you just need to put yourself out there. My approach is a little different, in that I believe there is a lot more that goes into manifesting love than just "putting yourself out there." I believe that you must honor who you are. That's a nonnegotiable. That's how you'll manifest the person you need. To show up as yourself may feel extremely different from all the pretending, masquerading, and imposter syndrome-ing you've done in the past. But this is important because half of knowing you found your man is feeling at home with him, and you cannot feel at home with your man if you are not at home with yourself. And you'll know when you've found that relaxed state with the right man if you are being 100 percent raw and honest with yourself from the start.

My goal for you is to learn how to listen to yourself, love yourself, trust yourself, and follow your own lead. Your intuition is your compass—it will never steer you wrong. I am going to teach you how to strengthen your intuitive muscle, heal from your past, and practice self-love. For The Universe to do its job of making a magical and true connection happen, self-love must be the most important aspect of the equation. You see, The Universe really does respond to you. Specifically, it responds to your most powerful wish. If you haven't done the work of getting to know yourself, then your wishes cannot authentically represent who you are and what you want.

"Love myself?" my clients say. "Sure, I'm good."

"Good is good," I say. "But, Chica, I want to hear you shouting from the rooftops that you love yourself. I want you exuding self-love from every glowing pore of your body, that very special all-inclusive golden love that we call *unconditional!*"

Love yourself beyond "I'm good," and your great and true love will find you. Once you begin to put out into the world your so-much-better-than-good wish—to be seen, known, and loved for who you truly are—you will no longer be interested in trying to change yourself to fit every random glass stiletto you stumble upon when leaving a party. You'll know who you are, that you are extraordinary, and that someone is out there who will love you for *everything* that you are (in all of your glorious imperfection).

In order for you to heal your past, you need to take an honest look at what truly has been holding you back from love. In *MAN*ifesting*, I'll introduce the Seven Dating Personas, and then chapter by chapter we'll explore a different one. These seven personas are patterns we've developed to protect ourselves from getting hurt. You've likely tried on each of them at some point in your dating life! These personas represent our fears and contribute to what blocks us from true love. Maybe you'll see yourself in many of them.

Though each dating persona manifests in different ways, at their core, each one is rooted in the same fear—that, yet again, this relationship won't work out and that you'll be disappointed one more time. This fear drives how you move into the next relationship, and the next, and the next...

But here's the golden ticket, the secret, the key to finding your man. Those fears are all based on *lies*. Each of these personas is based off the idea that you aren't good enough or worthy enough to be in a relationship full of love. The TRUTH is that you are *more* than worthy of love, and once you embrace how love-worthy you are, you'll open the floodgates and turn on your beacon to attract the kind of love you deserve.

I understand that getting past the fear and the repeated relationship patterns (what I will refer to as refrains) can be an exhausting process. And by understand, I mean I lived in those dating trenches. There was a time during my single years when I stopped talking to my mom about every single guy I was dating. I told her, "When there's something exciting to tell you, I'll let you know." My mom wanted what was best for me, of course. She wanted me to be happy and knew that part (OK, *all*) of me wanted what she and my dad have—a solid, lifelong, soul-connected bond and marriage. I thought that fending her off until I met a man who even came *close* to being a decent prospect would allow me to relax a bit, but she couldn't help herself. She would still ask, "Jay, any interesting men out there I should know about?"

There was no point in telling my mom about my awful date with "Narcissistic Nate" or my upcoming date with "Potentially The One Peter." When you are in dating mode, you never know how the next date will go, and sometimes it's hard to keep the faith. Talking with my mom about dating upset me, because it felt like her well-intentioned support and advice were slightly "off." Her striving to see my happily ever after stressed me out and sometimes caused me to be The Settler (the persona where you convince yourself that this guy is good enough because other people in your life love him or the idea of the two of you).

I also avoided talking about my dates with my mom because everything my mom knew about dating was based on her own experience, which was (a) of an entirely different generation and (b) limited, in that she married my dad, her college sweetheart whom she had known since grammar school. Things have changed out there. I'm sure I don't need to tell you that. I recently introduced my mom to the term "ghosting." She was appalled.

Turns out some of our happily ever after fantasies haven't updated with our technology. We need to recognize that our love stories are going to look very different from those of generations past. Many of today's love stories start on apps, on social media, and yes, in person too. There is no one set path anymore. Today's happily ever after stories lead us down many different paths. It's time to chuck the "I meet him at a party, he takes me to dinner, we meet his parents, he gets down on one knee, and we're married with two children by the time we're twenty-eight" path.

One of the best ways to get on the path to MAN*ifesting your man is to let go of your ideas of how it *should* happen. Don't be like Jenna, fixated on one path, one way to meet or not meet, or you'll shut down all the many unique and abundant ways that The Universe is trying to bring to you what you desire.

After several months of working with Jenna, helping her let go of her ideas about how her love story *should* look, sure enough I convinced her to join a few apps to just see what happens. Six weeks in, she met Trevor, who swept her off her feet and gave her a love story she'll be telling for the rest of her life despite the fact it started on a dating app. Speaking of meeting men through modern technology...

MAN*IFESTING MY HUSBAND

From as far back as I can remember, I imagined my life with my future husband on the daily. I wholeheartedly believed that it was going to happen for me, until I got to the point where I was doing everything possible to meet him, but it still wasn't happening. Something had to change. There was a lot I needed to learn, not that I was doing anything "wrong" but that my internal world needed a major upgrade. All this time, unbeknownst to me, I'd been manifesting the wrong guys for me. My mindset, negative narratives, misbeliefs, and unrealistic expectations were attracting the wrong men, and I wasn't allowing The Universe to bring me my man. I was in my own way.

After a series of relationships and "situationships" that were going nowhere, I was ready to throw my hands in the air and throw the towel in. I was very social, attending every possible event: every birthday party, every fundraiser, and every dinner I was invited to—just in case my man was there. Still, my man was nowhere to be found. Next, I researched all the dating sites (this was 2011—there were no dating apps), and I put myself on all of them!

I found Bryan on Match.com. Whoa, was he a looker. He was hot, athletic, and tall; had a great job; and seemed like a good man. I wrote to him. I had no problem writing to guys because my reasoning was trifold: there's a chance he just hasn't seen my profile, because he would've reached out; guys are busy and don't spend as much time on the sites, so he would appreciate me reaching out to him; and I'm happy to make the first move, and then he can take it from there. I used my standard message.

> *Hey [Bryan, in this case],*
>
> *You seem like a sweet, smart, laid-back, and fun guy. I'd love to know more about you. How's your week going so far?*
>
> *—Jaime*

Bryan wrote back the next day. We went back and forth for a few days until he asked me out for that Saturday night. He suggested meeting at an upscale sports bar/restaurant at 6:00 p.m. I accepted and was thrilled, but six o'clock on a Saturday night for drinks? Did that mean that he had plans after? Why so early? (I found out he didn't have plans after.) And a sports bar? That meant I couldn't wear my lucky first date little black dress…or could I?

I showed up in my LBD and told him I had a party to go to after the date (gotta be creative like that, and I did have an event if I chose to go). He looked just as handsome as he did in his pictures—a plus and a relief. The conversation flowed. He seemed like a down-to-earth, wholesome, smart guy from a good family.

At the end of the four hours, we parted ways. I had a wonderful time with him, but he didn't ask when we could spend time together again, and he didn't kiss me. We had such a great date, and no kiss! He did text me later on asking how the party was. I told him it was fun. I didn't tell him that I ended up not going anywhere but home after, because I wanted to relish in the amazing date I just had. I thanked him for the drinks, and we went back and forth a few times about how we both had a nice time together. Even though it was just the first date, I hadn't felt that excited about a guy since Ben (you'll hear about him later!).

Bryan was a consultant, working in North Carolina during the week and sometimes over weekends, so his travel schedule kept him from wanting to start anything serious until he was in Chicago again full time. We progressed very slowly—five dates in five months. I had to wait a whole month between the first and second date to kiss him, and to me, the kiss is how you know that you have a connection with a man. It was torture. But the kiss was incredible, and Bryan began to check off a lot of boxes in my book. I could be completely myself with him; he was intelligent, good looking, respectful, chill (I needed a chill man because my exes were not chill), thoughtful, and we had fun together. Also, he loved sports, which was very attractive to me. I'm guessing it's because I grew up with my dad and two brothers who loved sports, so it's what I wanted in my man. Do I love sports? Not so much, but I wanted my man to love sports. Bryan played soccer in college, so that was a huge plus. I had BIG feelings for this man!

After every incredible date, he would say "goodbye." There was no "When can I see you again?" He was the biggest game player without trying to be a game player. He was oblivious. He had no idea it was making me crazy, but all I could do was trust, which is what I did. I would tell myself that if we were supposed to continue seeing each other, we would. I was practicing having no attachment to the outcome, which I teach my clients now. On the fourth date, he asked me if I wanted to spend New Year's Eve with him, and I was ecstatic.

That eve we became exclusive. Bryan thought we already were, but I told him that anything goes until you have that conversation. I had no idea that he felt that way, and I learned that he wasn't the best communicator, but he was cute, so he got away with it. I had been dating other guys up until that point—because I didn't know how he had felt.

After we got into the groove of things, we started having even more fun. I would plan a whole day and night of surprise venues and activities, and then he would do the same. Six months into our relationship, he blindfolded me and took me to an arboretum to tell me he loved me. I said it back. I surprised him with a trip to the aquarium and planetarium, and we continued exchanging secret adventures and saying, "I love you." It was fun to be tourists in our own city and meld into each other's lives. I lived above a karaoke bar, and I love to sing, so every night that we were together, at the end of the night, we would stop in so I could sing a song or two. Bryan is not interested in singing, but he loved watching me do my thing. We met each other's families and friends and did all the things lovers do in the honeymoon phase. I was in love, on a high, and never wanted to come down.

Our relationship wasn't perfect. There was a learning curve of getting used to each other. We both got better at communicating when something was bothering us. I used my psychological tools to help with things. We would discuss if there were judgments and then discuss that they only kept us disconnected, so we would try and understand each other more. I practiced gratitude, and instead of complaining or wishing he was different, I would accept him for all he was. Acceptance is the first law of spirituality. I looked at him as a human, not perfect, just like me. This was big for me because, before him, I may or may not have cut guys off for things that weren't a big deal. I was growing in this relationship.

After almost two years of dating, Bryan proposed. I had imagined that moment my whole life, and it finally happened. He had sent me on a scavenger hunt around the city of Chicago and told me to pack a bag. (I packed a suitcase.) Every place I went (mostly restaurants) would have a card and a rose waiting for me. I felt like Carrie from *Sex in the City*, hopping in and out of taxis in my cute pale-pink cocktail dress and heels, carrying roses, cards, and little gifts, accumulating more at each stop until I reached the Peninsula Hotel, where I was directed to the terrace. Bryan was there to greet me. He had my favorite love songs playing in the background, and he got down on one knee and proposed.

I screamed, "Yes!"

Of course I did, because I had MAN*ifested The One, and we were off to a wonderful start. But it did not come as easy as it was for you to read that little love story of a match made by The Universe. As you read this book, you will see how I learned and grew, how I healed, and how I resolved any unsettled issues in order to MAN*ifest The One. You will see how I work with women who are doing the same on their path to MAN*ifesting their man. And you will see how you can MAN*ifest your man too. Do the work on these pages, and The Universe will bring The One right to *you*, on your doorstop—or in your inbox.

MY PROMISE

I'm not gonna lie—getting honest with and about yourself in order to get the results you want takes work, courage, and willingness. But this is what I say to the women who come to me for guidance as they start their journey to love.

If you bear with me and trust me while we walk this path together, by the end of the journey, your amphibian-smooching days will be over—you will have found your prince. Standing at the threshold of a more encompassing love than you can imagine at this moment. You will feel at peace, knowing that you couldn't and wouldn't have wanted your path to veer any other way, because after meeting your man, everything that happened and everything you went through along your journey will ALL be worth it, and it will ALL make sense. You will have MAN*ifested, and you will never look back again.

I promise...

- You, the Gen Z Girl, just starting your search for "forever" love (so far, in all the wrong places).
- You, the Millennial, feeling like you've gone on a bazillion dates and still haven't found your man.
- You, Mrs. Married Woman, realizing your marriage lacks authenticity and true connection.
- You, Ms. Divorcée, now at long last, learning who you are and how to love yourself.

- You, Ms. Widow, who has gone through hell and back but still gently returns to the dating world to find love again even though you know that there will always be a place in your heart for your beloved.

This book and the path it lights is for each and every one of you. This book is for anyone willing to do the work of being unflinchingly honest, raw, and open. These pages contain the power to render you capable of manifesting a life full of love— the life that up until now you have only dreamed of. Let me help you make your dreams a reality.

As I've shared, *MAN*ifesting* covers all Seven Dating Personas and is filled with my personal stories and stories of the women I've worked with so that you have a reliable and relatable guide on the journey to self-love and the love of The One (a.k.a. your "Person"). In each chapter you will find an affirmation to move you forward on the journey and away from the past and negative narratives. But most importantly you'll find an exercise to complete at the end of the chapter, because learning something is OK, but *knowing* it and putting it into practice is how you integrate your learnings into your life.

I encourage you to have a journal for the journey—your MAN*ifesting journal! This will be one of the best tools along the way, even if you don't consider yourself a writer or have never journaled before. There is no right way to write down words. But know that when you do it, it is no longer stuck within you and that your journal will be a resource for all that you will learn and unlearn (i.e., old negative narratives) in these pages.

Before we dive into chapter 1 and the Seven Dating Personas, let's begin with a journal exercise.

INTRODUCTION EXERCISE: BE LOVE

#1: Take out your MAN*ifesting journal and open it to the first page. Think of someone who loved or loves you unconditionally. Someone, somewhere, at some point, loved you for exactly who you are, and you felt it, believed it, and knew it. Write down a few sentences about this person and your relationship. How did their love shape you, and what were you able to do with this love that you might not have been able to do if it had been withheld or nonexistent? This doesn't have to be a significant other; it could be a family member or friend.

#2: If you aren't comfortable or familiar (yet) with the notion of "unconditional love," call up a single loving moment you shared with someone. This person can be a grandparent, parent, sibling, teacher, friend, or even a non-person (a four-legged friend, for example). If the idea of writing about such love still escapes you, write about a place where you feel most at peace.

#3: Now, fully let go and allow yourself to explore the emotions surrounding this person, place, or thing. What did it feel like to be so loved? Where were you? What was it about this person or experience that made you feel loved? Was it their words, actions, essence, or just "knowing"? Write down as much as you can about this love.

#4: If you feel like you truly haven't experienced unconditional love yet (yet is a key word here, because you will experience unconditional love before you know it), then do your best to imagine what it would feel like to be enveloped in the arms

of love with no judgment—someone loving you NO MATTER WHAT! Would it feel warm, peaceful, safe, joyful, empowering, beautiful? Jot down emotions in words and phrases. Practice using these words and phrases, and try visualizing how it would feel to be bathed in them.

#5: After you have written your last word, close your eyes and stay in this soulful, open space for a moment. Vow to carry these feelings and related memories of the experiences with you as a daily reminder that you are loved. If it helps, take one word or phrase with you—maybe on a Post-it or a note tucked into your wallet or jewelry box. Even if the person you've written about is no longer living or is no longer in your life, you know what it's like to feel loved.

#6: Repeat this journal exercise when you are feeling lost and before each and every date or first encounter so that you can get into that place of feeling love, being loved, and knowing that you're unconditionally lovable.

CHAPTER ONE

I Am Not Worthy
Versus I Am Enough

Affirmation: "I forgive myself and love myself no matter what, with no judgment. I trust in myself, and I know that I am beyond worthy of love."

EVERY STORY HOLDS POTENTIALLY transformative power. Through language, we can connect, inspire, educate, motivate, heal, leave an impact, and make dreams come true. How we speak to and about ourselves—in daily conversations with others or alone in front of the mirror before going on a date—has a profound impact on who and what we attract. If the pre-date message we tell ourselves is, "I doubt this guy is going to like me. He's probably dating women much hotter than me, like perfect women with porcelain skin. Look at this zit on my chin. I'm a mess," then we are going to show up to the date a mess. On the other hand, if the message is, "I'm really excited for this guy to get to know me because I'm going to let my amazing, fun, smart, and beautiful light shine," then that's what he will see—the authentic and fabulous you.

"I'll never find my man. All the good guys are already taken."

When we say that out loud or in our head, The Universe takes note, and because like attracts like, this supposed "man shortage" becomes real—it manifests. A cycle of "I'll never—" and "Woe is me" begins, and it will become increasingly harder to escape. Another good guy snatched up will be "proof" there is no hope. On the other hand, if we shout from our very heart and soul, "I'm enough and I believe there is enough love for every single *single* out here," The Universe is going to embrace us. The Universe will hear our wild, empowered call, and like a Sherpa, it will guide us toward abundance and to the pinnacle of everything that is possible. At this pinnacle, we will find our true, authentic love.

But of course, even the best Sherpas in the world cannot carry us up the mountain. We have to prepare, warm up, become familiar with the path, and then put one foot in front of the other to start our journey. Simply put: We have to do the work first, the work of paying attention and listening. What are the covert and overt messages we receive, from our formative early girlhood years on, from parents, teachers, friends, family, strangers, and society at large? We want to explore these messages because they all contribute to the collectively limiting beliefs we hold about ourselves. Once we understand that these limiting beliefs shape us just as much as we shape (and reshape) them, we can begin to move from self-judging messages (*I suck*) toward self-compassionate ones (*Wow! I'm a beautiful being who deserves love and who has so much love to give*).

We can literally use words to heal past wounds and unearth untruths about ourselves and our world. We can then turn ourselves in any direction we please. True love awaits each of us—as long as we send the signal and clear the way. We begin this book by learning how to positively project what is already inside of you, so that you can begin to act as a beacon of light to The Universe and to your man.

WHAT'S YOUR STORY?

Life is hard. Love is harder. Or do we make it so? Countless stories of love and romance don't align with the realities and nuances of being a single woman in the twenty-first century. Thanks to so many fairy tales and rom-coms, women are fixated with their own love stories looking a certain way. No wonder love is harder. Women are pressured to be married by a certain age, to beat the biological clock that keeps on ticking, and to meet the expectations of constant romance and endless walks on the beach at sunset. Women tell themselves that in order to find The One they must be where the men are and that they must make themselves the perfect cocktail of available and hard to get. We, as women, tend to go a little crazy trying to achieve these relationship goals. Meanwhile, there's the terrified voice in the back of our head screaming on repeat, "But what if I never meet him?"

At the root of this fear is the story that many women tell themselves—you aren't good enough the way you are. You're not skinny, funny, pretty, independent, intelligent, attractive, successful, calm, quiet, creative...enough. Yet when we get to the heart of the matter, attracting the man of our dreams is not about how available or unavailable we seem or where we are in the game of life; the real work is an inside job. Women must recognize who they authentically are and celebrate that all women are all 100 percent worthy of love.

Manifesting love is not for the faint of heart; however, it doesn't need to be as difficult as some people make it out to be. All you need are willingness, clarity, and a great deal of courage and strength of heart. Oh, you also need openness, vulnerability, trust, and self-love, but you already know that.

I acknowledge you for your willingness to go out and get what you deserve, what you came to this earth for; it's your birthright to find the right one for you and it WILL happen!

While popular culture may shout (in a fear-inducing tone) the prevalence of hooking up, the rise in divorce rates, and the impossibility of finding a dream match, the quieter truth is that love is everywhere. We all seek love if we don't feel we have it, and when we do have it, most of us consciously work on ways to make it stronger, deeper, and more authentic. Over twenty years after Cher sang her way back into the global consciousness, asking if we all "believe in life after love," we continue to prove that not only do we believe in life after love, but we believe in love after love too! We heal. We don't give up after heartbreak. We are resilient, and love itself makes us so.

I wrote this book because I know how seekers of true love and marriage feel, because not only was I that woman, but she's in the hundreds of clients I see day in and day out. Women who are lying in bed at night, wondering what is wrong with them, wondering why hasn't the love that has found so many others shown up for them. Women who are lonely, which is further causing them to retreat, their self-confidence shattered. Women whose minds reel with all the "wrong moves" they've made in the past—trying to figure out how and when they messed up their one shot at love. In the quiet moments of their day, these women shed tears, wondering what the secret to love is and, more importantly, why no one has let them in on it.

MAN*ifesting is here to reveal the secret to finding love.

In fact, we do not just have ONE shot at love. We do not live in a world where The Universe says, "Oh well, you fell in love, and it didn't work out for you; maybe the next lifetime you'll have love." Thinking that they blew it, that they only had one chance, keeps women stuck in the patterns of the past. If it was supposed to work out with Luke or Jeremy or Ryan or...then it would have. Ruminating over the past is not a good look. A woman must be present to manifest her future to manifest her man. Her man is waiting and wanting to meet her just as much as she's waiting and wanting to meet him.

I am about empowerment, giving women the means and the resources within to HEAL from the past and show up authentically to attract the real love they deserve.

Grounded wholly in the notion that The Universe has our backs, *MAN*ifesting* reconnects you with the playfulness, hope, and youthful determination that fueled your early years, turning the quest to MAN*ifest your man into an enlivening experience rather than one filled with angst and pressure. It's all about your attitude. Dating not only can be fun, but it also should be fun. Finding The One is not a linear tale of love peppered with glass slippers, magic carpets, and meet-cutes but a messy winding adventure of finding your way.

MAN*ifesting will guide your discovery of your own inner strength and authentic empowerment, and it will encourage you to connect with the powerfully playful loving heart that beats inside every woman, a heart that once truly open and set free will bring all you desire into your life and more.

I want you to know yourself and to *know* your man is out there.

NO MATTER WHAT

When you were a little kid and you imagined yourself in a relationship as an adult, how did you see it? Did you imagine yourself happy, having fun, laughing, and crying together with your husband? Did you imagine more happy days together than sad? Did you imagine growing and thriving together?

Whatever you imagined your ideal relationship to be, you can have it because you didn't come to this earth to NOT have a relationship that feels joyful and instills peace in your heart. When and why did you lose sight of your destiny and your truth? I don't care what anyone says. Love *is* the basis of life. Loving and feeling loved is EVERYTHING. Love makes us feel good—mind, body, soul.

You have a choice, and you can manifest and create the love you deserve versus settling and not being an active participant in your life. You have the power to cultivate your ideal relationship; there's no reason why you can't have what you desire and deserve.

We can't find true, authentic love unless we know we're worthy of it. Manifesting love needs to start with becoming aware of the stories you're telling yourself and then examining them to discover their origin. Did a boy in the sandbox in preschool tell you you're ugly? Did you grow up with a parent who loved you with conditions, as in only when you did something "good," like getting an *A* on a test or winning the gold medal at your gymnastics competition? Did you have a boyfriend who made you feel unworthy of love? When things aren't going well in our love lives and we have had some negative experiences in our past (everyone does), everything else seems to fall apart, but you don't need to be a victim of your circumstances.

If you identify as a victim and that's what you are focused on, The Universe will bring you more reasons to feel like a victim. Start identifying as resilient and thriving, and The Universe will bring you more experiences and opportunities for you to thrive.

Life happens *for* us, not *to* us. There are learning opportunities in all of our experiences. You can choose to think that life is unfair, that you've been dealt a "bad hand." Or you can do your best to be in acceptance of what is and do whatever is in your power to change the trajectory of the rest of your life, taking your beautiful learnings and wisdom with you. Your past doesn't need to be a determiner of your present or your future. You have the power to change your lens of perception and change that negative narrative in your mind.

The problem is that many women are walking around completely unaware of how detrimental these narratives are. Once you become aware of the negative narratives you can do something about them. Just like someone with an addiction who enters rehab, you have to first admit that there is a problem. Our outside experiences reflect our inner reality, meaning that you need to love yourself unconditionally in order to bring in (through the law of attraction) your perfect match, your *bashert* (destiny), your soulmate, your "Person." Think back to the guys you dated in the past. What was going on inside of you? Were you filled with doubt, fear, and insecurities? If so, it will make sense when you think of the men who showed up—guys who validated those insecurities. So, you see why it's crucial to start being kind and gentle with yourself.

The Self-Negator is always telling themselves bad news. "Another good guy gone means none left for me. When he doesn't call, it's because I'm a loser."

It's time to talk to yourself the way you talk to your loved ones—with kindness. You have to stop beating yourself up.

The negative messages and unkind voices contribute to the collectively limiting beliefs that we hold about ourselves. However, once we understand that these limiting beliefs shape us just as much as we shape (and reshape) them, we can begin to move from self-negating messages (*I suck*) toward self-celebratory ones (*Wow! I'm a beautiful being who deserves love and who has so much love to give!*).

If we shout from our very heart and soul, "I'm enough, and I believe there is enough love for every single, *single* out here," The Universe will hear our call, and like a Sherpa, it will guide us toward our true authentic love. Adopt an "abundance mindset" versus a "scarcity mindset." Your love is waiting and wanting to meet you just as much as you want to meet him.

I'm sure you've heard that you have to love yourself before you can be loved (the way you deserve to be loved), and I'm sure you've rolled your eyes because it sounds cliché. Like something that people say just to say it because they have no better response to your complaints that you haven't found your "person" yet. Not to mention, it can be offensive to hear. Why would someone make such an assumption that you don't love yourself? I'm here to show you its importance, and I'll break it down for you in a way that makes sense.

Unconditionally loving yourself is the first and most crucial aspect to MAN*ifesting. *What does unconditionally loving yourself mean, and why it is so important?* It means that you love yourself NO MATTER WHAT. It means that you have forgiven yourself, hold no judgment, love all aspects, and accept yourself as you are.

Unconditional self-love seems easy enough, but the problem is that women are walking around unaware of the negative narratives running through their minds on loop, and these negative narratives are holding them back from manifesting love. The reason why it's so important to love yourself unconditionally is because The Universe will bring to you a reflection of what's going on inside of you. If you are feeling bad about yourself because of your past relationships or something one of your parents said to you when you were a child that you believed, then your internal world will be reflecting just that.

ANNA, THE SELF-NEGATOR

I received a voicemail from a prospective client named Anna. I could tell in her voice that she was hesitant and a bit resistant.

"Hi, my name is Anna and, um, I would like to set up a session with you—I mean that's if you're taking new clients. You're probably not, but if you happen to be, then please call me back at"—she left her phone number—"but if you're too busy, you could just email me or just text me, but you probably won't get back to me for a while, so I'll just be patient. No rush! If you can't get back to me, no worries, I'll be OK!"

It was clear that this girl needed to work on loving herself, respecting herself, and knowing her worth. She just assumed that there wouldn't be a spot for her in my practice. I called her back, and we set up an appointment for her (to her surprise).

Anna's parents divorced before she could walk. She doesn't remember a time when her dad lived in her house. Now she was a thirty-year-old dermatologist. She reported having a wonderful relationship with her dad in our first session. He was loving and supportive, and even though she didn't live with him all the time (she lived with her mom in the burbs, and her dad lived in the city, so she saw him every other weekend), he showed up to every dance show, every concert she sang in, and every soccer game she played.

So, we established that she had a secure attachment with her father and felt unconditionally loved by him. Now, here's the hard and frustrating part of the human condition. As humans we have a negativity bias. Meaning that we can be loved by a hundred people and unloved by one, but we will focus on that one who doesn't love us, and we will believe that we are unlovable. This was Anna's issue.

Anna's mother, who was her primary caregiver, was an alcoholic who wasn't happy in her own life, so she projected her anger and unhappiness onto Anna. Anna was her mother's little punching bag so to speak. Because her mother didn't feel good about herself, she would insult Anna, and not only that, her mother was constantly putting herself down. She was modeling the opposite of self-love.

In our sessions, Anna would tell me story after story that displayed this detrimental behavior. If she wasn't telling Anna to lose weight because "boys don't like fat girls," she was complaining to Anna about how she feels like she is ugly, unsexy, and disgusting. That's why she can't land a man, and that's why Anna's father left. (There was NO ownership with that lady—just pure blaming and projecting.) Anna's father left her mother because she couldn't stay sober and wasn't willing to do anything about it. So, here is Anna in my office going on and on about how she "sucks" and feels horrible about herself. She is fully aware of the fact that she isn't kind to herself, but she had no idea how destructive it was to her finding love.

I explained to Anna that how she sees herself is how the world will see her, and more specifically how men see her. I asked if she was willing to do the work to heal the years of emotional and verbal abuse from her mother.

"Of course, I want to heal, but I don't see how it's possible. I will always hate my mom for effing up my life."

I replied, "If that's what you think, then that's what will happen, but if you're open to healing your past and learning how to love yourself, I am here to support and help you navigate your healing journey. Many women have come before you and showed up to the do the work and have healed and moved on to find their 'person.' He is out there, somewhere. He is literally doing something right now. Maybe he is on his lunch break and chatting with friends, or maybe he is on a business call, or what if he is at his therapy session talking about how he is finally ready to settle down? Anna, you have to get out of your own way. In life, the same thing is going to keep happening over and over unless you make a change. I understand and I hear you, that you are angry and you resent your mom, and I hear you. That had a *huge* negative impact on your life up until now, but you have a choice now. You can let her treatment toward you dictate the rest of your life, or you can choose to take your life back. You can know the truth about you, and whenever your ego (mind) starts to tell you lies, you need to tell it to please quiet down because they are just lies, based on the projections of your mom, who needed a punching bag. Holding on to your anger will only keep you where you are—the land of negativity."

Silence.

Anna glanced out the window, likely in deep contemplation. After a few minutes, I saw a single tear roll down her cheek.

"See this!" She sat up straight, looked at me with conviction, and pointed to the lone tear. "This is the last tear that I am going to shed because of my past. You're right. I am keeping myself in the jail of my past, and I want to set myself free. My negative thoughts about myself or life don't deserve my energy. My mom doesn't deserve my energy. My past doesn't deserve my energy. If I don't want to die alone, I can't keep going on like this."

"Exactly, Anna! Our thoughts create our reality. It sounds like you are ready to start thinking, feeling, and being more positive, yes?"

"Absolutely. I realize now that I have the power to manifest. I was holding myself back, and I'm done now.

Anna and I formulated an experiment for her that was very "Pavlov's dogs-esque" in nature. She liked the idea of wearing a hair tie or scrunchie on her wrist at all times. Whenever she would think something negative, like *I'm never going to meet my man*, or *OMG, I'm loving this guy, what are the chances that he is going to love me back?* Anna was supposed to snap her band and then replace the thought with a positive one.

"OK, so say I'm walking down the street, and I see a couple holding hands and laughing." She was excited about this experiment. "Instead of getting depressed about it and saying to myself that that kind of love isn't available for me, I will say to myself,

'What an inspiration. I can't wait to experience that for myself when the time is right!'"

"Yes, you got it, Anna!"

These things take time. This is rewiring your brain, but the great news is that our brains can experience neuroplasticity. Even though they have been operating a certain way for a long time, by actively doing this, you can create new pathways for your brain that result in a naturally more positive way of thinking. At the beginning and through the process, rewiring takes a lot of conscious effort, but it is worth it in the end when you get to the point where you naturally think positively, where you will find the world changing around you, and where all things seem easier. There is less drama, and you feel inner peace because you're not working hard to fight and stay safe; you are just operating from your natural state which *is* positive and loving. Here you start to attract better quality men into your life.

Anna took this work to heart and began her journey to authentic empowerment. She stayed diligent with her weekly sessions. She was honest about her frustration with her progress. I reiterated that it takes time and that she should be gentle with herself. Her brain has been operating a certain way for a *long* time, so it takes some time to rewire. Luckily the timeline rule for a breakup doesn't apply here. You know the one. It goes something like this: however long your relationship was, it takes you half that amount of time to heal and recover from it (assuming it was an unwanted breakup). This work doesn't need to take a year or even six months when you stay on top of things, remaining conscious and connected with yourself.

A few weeks went by, and I could tell that things were really starting to shift for Anna. She reported feeling more joyful and optimistic. She came into my office for her regular Thursday 4:30 p.m. session with a massive perma-smile on her face.

"Remember I told you I was going to that dermatology conference?" she asked, sitting down in her usual chair.

I nodded.

"I met an incredible man there. Dr. Michael Hunter. I mean, even his name is hot!"

"OK, so now that we know he is hot, tell me more about him, and more importantly, tell me what was going on internally when you met him."

"Michael is thirty-four, he is obviously smart, and he is sweet and funny," Anna chirped on. "He comes from a great family. He is attentive and gives me tons of compliments. He loves sports, he is genuine, and I know that I just met him, but there is something that is *so* different about this man and how I am with him. I am confident. I don't worry if he is going to contact me because I have no attachment to the outcome. I am trusting The Universe, and I am trusting *myself* that I have everything inside I need to have a loving relationship."

"Who are you, and what did you do with Anna?" I replied.

"I know! Can you believe it?"

"Of course, I can believe it, because I've always known that you could conquer your Self-Negator ways. It was *you* that needed to believe in yourself, my dear."

Anna went on to date "Dr. Wonderful" for the duration of the time she was in therapy. It was an honor to witness her continued transformation and growth. Every week she became stronger and more connected with her essential inner true nature who loved herself unconditionally and was full of confidence and joie de vivre.

Two years later on a Thursday evening, as I was going through my work emails, I came across a message from Anna that was sent at 4:30 p.m. Was it a coincidence, or was it The Universe affirming that Anna had done the work and found her way? In the email, Anna told me that she and Michael had got engaged and would be getting married that summer. She said that she has never felt more at peace, happy, and excited about life. She couldn't wait to spend the rest of her life with her "person." She told me that unfortunately her mother had gotten cancer, but through her journey back to health, they had become closer because she forgave her and finally found the compassion within for her mother. She closed her email by thanking me for helping her make life-changing leaps and bounds toward the person she was meant to be that led her to the person she was meant to be with.

My heart was bursting, in the way that a parent feels when their child has accomplished something they had thought was insurmountable and impossible but then it becomes a reality. In many ways, my clients are like children to me. I get to watch them grow and evolve, and it's a true honor every time.

FORGIVE YOURSELF, AND GET OUT OF YOUR OWN WAY

At the end of the day, you are the only one who is holding you back from receiving love. It's no one's fault that you haven't (yet) brought in the love you deserve. It's not your ex's fault for ending the relationship, and it's not your fault that you haven't been ready yet. As long as you keep beating yourself up over your choices, it will never be productive, and it's certainly not a healthy way to exist. Forgive yourself and remind yourself that you have always been doing the best you can. This will help you be open and make that shift into loving and having compassion for yourself. The law of attraction teaches that when we love ourselves, love will be attracted to us.

Life is hard, and there are so many things that are out of our control. In a world where control is simply an illusion, at least we can get empowered, and we can get ahold of ourselves—to change the narrative in our minds. Once you start believing, knowing, and feeling that you deserve love, feeling and thinking in a positive way will become second nature, and everything will fall into place. An unexpected "chance" meeting in a park or a coffee shop might turn into an innocent conversation, which could turn into a date, which just might just turn into twenty dates, an engagement, and a beautiful marriage. You just NEVER know when you're going to meet your "person," so make sure that you are doing everything possible to not give The Universe *any* reason to not bring your love forward. It's going to happen if you believe it's going to happen.

CHAPTER ONE EXERCISE: BE SELF-COMPASSIONATE

Learn to love yourself with compassionate forgiveness. Forgive yourself and stop judging what you have done or what you do. You have the permission to be kinder and gentler with yourself. You have the means to release the misbeliefs and misidentifications that have had you in a stronghold.

#1: Time to get out your MAN*ifesting journal. Identify a negative narrative or limiting belief that you have been telling yourself. Write it down in the journal. An example: "I don't feel like I am deserving of love."

#2: Read your negative narrative or limiting belief aloud. Identify where the story comes from. Does it originate from a parent? An ex? Who or what situation instated this belief in you? Write down whatever comes forward into your awareness.

#3: Put your hand on your heart as you ask yourself: What is the truth? Close your eyes. Keep your eyes closed until it comes to you. An example: "The truth is that I am deserving of love. It is my birthright to have love in my life." Proclaim your truth out loud. Another example: "I forgive myself for buying into the misbelief that I'm unlovable, unworthy, or incapable of having the love I desire." Take a deep breath and let the truth settle in. Embody the truth. Let it flow through your entire consciousness.

#4: Go back to your journal. Write down your truth. Cross out your negative story or limiting belief.

CHAPTER TWO

Back to the Source—
Our Playful Inner Child

Affirmation: "*I will show up authentically in life because I know who I am, and who I am is beautiful inside and out. My person will love me for all that I am no matter what, and I can't wait to meet the love of my life.*"

EVERYONE AND THEIR MOTHER is touting the value of being authentic these days, but authenticity is not a buzzword or trend. The practice of searching for and finding your deepest, most genuine self and then listening to and acting from that space contains timeless wisdom and healing power. Woman power starts as girl power, and girl power is the sheer joy, lightheartedness, and freedom you experienced as a child that originated from various outlets—family relationships, friends, or childhood hobbies and activities that you loved and brought you joy.

Keeping this wonder and awe with you throughout your life is a magical way to live, and I highly recommend it. Still, authenticity isn't always as easy as it seems, especially if our authentic ways have been stuffed away for years. Society teaches us to fit in with everyone else and to redirect our true desires if they aren't "cool" enough. It can take a while to shed our pretending ways, which is why it is incredibly easy to take on the dating persona of The Chameleon. Like Julia Roberts in *Runaway Bride*, you continuously alter who you are, or what you like, to be accepted by the one you want to love you. But pretending will only end in heartache. True love requires that you show up and show him who you are at your core.

Our authentic self, otherwise known as our soul, is deeply rooted in who we were as kids, more specifically who we were when we came into this world. Somehow, it got lost in the mix at some point, and it's dying to shine again—just like the little girl within you. No one will ever be able to get close to you and be intimate with you until you are intimate with yourself. The better you get at sitting with and becoming you fully, right here and right now, the better your best match will be able to find you. The better everything will be.

The One finds those who love themselves, feel worthy, and are ready for love. So, wake up your true self, let her shine, and get ready for that light to guide you to the person you've been looking for. This chapter gets you back in touch with who you really are.

A fundamental part of MAN*ifesting is learning how to become a whole person, rather than showing up expecting and hoping that your man will complete you. The love you share will add to the already whole you—it's like the icing on the cake. You don't want to be half-baked when you meet your guy. You want to be fully cooked and steaming hot (pun intended!).

The truth is it's not always so easy to reconnect to our wholeness, but by practicing connection with the little girl within, you can get there. Your life will feel lighter, you will experience more joy and more freedom, and then it won't be long before your eyes see more clearly, your heart will be fuller, and your energy will be more open to bringing in your "person."

One way that I connect with "little Jaime" is through my childhood joy of singing. If I go too long without belting out some Mariah or Celine in the shower (excellent acoustics—I highly recommend it!), I feel less alive. There is a simplicity and beauty in being as open, open-minded, and vulnerable as we were in our youth. If we can remember that we all started in the sandbox—as equals, as lovable and loving children with infinite potential—we can realize our birthright. Hey, if I can continue to get excited over my dreams and ambitions as I used to in the sandbox, then I can do anything, including finding true love.

When I was thirteen, one of my dreams came true. I got to play Annie in *Little Orphan Annie*. I was in eighth grade, and I'll never forget the day I found out the news. I was at the mall with my best friend, Abby, and when my dad picked us up, he told me. Tears of joy, excitement, and disbelief ran down my face. I was thrilled. Why am I bringing this up in a book about manifesting your man? I'm sharing this story because it is highly relevant to anyone who is MAN*ifesting. Reminding yourself of who you are and then showing up from that place is crucial in the MAN*ifesting process. Annie, to me, represents, in many ways, my essence. She shines! She goes after what she wants. She is feisty, sweet and kind, powerful, resilient, and most of all, she is POSITIVE, positive being the keyword here!

I popped into this world a ball of sparkling sunshine illuminating and spreading positivity wherever I went—that was me until life experiences and relationships got in the way, my light dimmed, and my positive attitude turned a little cynical. The demise of my shine was a mixture of disappointments, challenging times, and guys who seemed promising but didn't work out. I was taking setbacks and rejection to mean something about me, but that couldn't be further from the truth (I know this fact now, but back then, it hurt…a lot). Back then, I stockpiled these experiences instead of letting them go. I started to identify with them rather than holding what I knew deep inside to be true about me.

When I was a little girl and had a bad day, I would tell myself, "Jaime, this day sucks, but you'll feel better within the next week," and I ALWAYS did. However, it became increasingly difficult to experience that as life went on. I'm guessing that you, my beloved reader, can relate. They say little kids, little problems, big kids, big problems. I thought that my positive attitude and quick turnaround from pain would last forever, but as an adult, my perspective started to feel more like "fuhgeddaboudit!"

Through my studies of psychology, social work, spiritual psychology, and plenty of therapy along the way, I learned a lot about healing, and that's what I'm here to teach and inspire in you. There is one thing I know now (it took me a long time to get here), and I want you to know this too—and live it.

Pain is temporary, and healing is always possible.

MAN*ifesting is about you returning to the soul you were born as—no matter what life has thrown at you. I know you might be thinking that it feels impossible because you haven't seen her in a long time, but not only is it possible, it's the second step to manifesting love.

The little girl inside is still there—talk to her, tell her that she has always been doing the best she could. Tell her you have her back but also listen to her wisdom as she is wise and has things to say to you about yourself that you may have forgotten.

It's natural to abandon the little girl within because perhaps you wanted to leave her in the past because of any previous negative experiences or relationships you had, but that's backwards thinking. The truth is that part of healing, growing, evolving, and maturing is the act of merging the little girl with the you of today. She is part of you, a beautiful, sweet, and innocent part of you who has been through A LOT. Tell her you are so proud of her for all she has been through. Let her know that you are a team and can rely on each other as you go on with the rest of your life.

I have an abundance of compassion for little Jaime. There were many times that I was put down or someone was "mean" to me, and even though my mom would always tell me that it was because they were jealous, I never believed her. Because regardless of what was going on with them, it still was painful. If only I had had the tools I have now, and if only I had loved myself then the way I love myself now, I could have avoided a lot of pain and suffering. And this is why it's essential to merge with your little self because she needs to be held and reminded of how incredible she is.

I remember in fourth grade I won the citizenship award. This award was granted because of votes from my peers. I was very humble and beyond excited that I had won. That afternoon, Tracy, a "friend" from class (more like a "frenemy" as they say these days) was over at my house. We were sitting in my room working on a puzzle when out of nowhere, she told me that Justin Forester only voted for me because he thought I was a dork...AND I BELIEVED HER! I was in love with Justin (and so was she), so to hear that, I was devastated. Tracy robbed my excitement of winning. Looking back, I can now think to myself: (a) Tracy, you're a "B" for sharing that (false) information with me, and (b) WTF, that's just not true, and it makes zero sense. I was so far from knowing how to love myself that I effing believed her. Hurt people, hurt people. Period.

It's important to get back to YOU because when you are MAN*ifesting you have to show up as your authentic self so that you can attract your match, the man who is completely aligned with your essence, your core, your truth, the real you—not the jaded one who is showing up currently, the insecure one who is playing games. The one whose walls are up and whose heart is closed. No, you need to show up with an open heart and walls collapsed to let love in. To let in this man who wants to know the real you, you'll need to let him in.

How do you get your authentic self back? You have to look at where you veered off the path. Do you ever look in the mirror and wonder where "you" have gone? That woman looking back at you is overwhelmed by life and disconnected from the energetic and hopeful spirit you had in your childhood. You have no idea how all of a sudden you are this adult when you swear you were just sitting in Mr. Green's eighth-grade science class, sending notes about your crush back and forth between you and your best friend. Yes, everyone grows up, matures, and feels like they don't identify with the child they once were. In fact, you might feel like that child is not really "you" anymore. Yet you have never been more YOU than when you were a child, as that is when you were your purest, most authentic self. That was before "life" happened.

I know it's unbelievable how fast time flies, but that is the reality. The reality is that as we get older, we have more and more life experiences that aren't all sunshine and rainbows, and it seems that with each occurrence we lose a piece of our child-like essence. The result is that we feel unfulfilled and unhappy, and we are surviving and not thriving. I'm here to tell you that you have the power to function as an adult but also bring that beautiful essence back, because it has always been there; you've just been ignoring it. That essence is your inner child. Your little one wants to play, likes to laugh, loves to run around, and does not want to worry about everything. Your little one is carefree and only wants to focus on the big picture of why we are all here on this planet—to enjoy life, learn lessons, and get to know ourselves as we are going through it. Increasing your happiness by connecting with your inner child is accessible to everyone. It takes a little energy and an attitude shift, but you will be good to go.

RELEASE THE CHAMELEON—SET YOURSELF FREE

The recipe for leaving The Chameleon behind happens by connecting with yourself and your inner child to really get to know the real you. When you don't have a solid foundation and you're not standing strong in who you are, what you stand for, and what you have to offer, it's easy to veer off the path and lose yourself. When you shed your Chameleon ways and start living your life for you, you will feel more empowered and powerful, and your inner child will feel more loved.

Children are incredibly innocent. Because of their lack of life experience, they have a minimal number of negative stories (if any) running through their minds every day, like some adults do. There has been less time to bring them down and suck the essence out of their soul. Children are clean slates. Their love is pure, and they are constantly open to receiving and giving love. If you want to feel love in your heart again, I recommend spending some time connecting with your inner child and feeling what it felt like as a kid, how open it was, and how happy love made you feel.

If you happen to have experienced any abuse or neglect in your childhood, or you experienced intense trauma, please know that it is healable. If your childhood wasn't innocent for whatever reason, you are not broken. You were born just like everyone else, an innocent, beautiful, unharmed soul. Picking up the pieces of your past and putting them back together is what this work is all about. As you heal you become and feel more whole again. If all you can remember from your childhood is negative memories, this might be the first time that you know what it's like to feel like your true self. Finding yourself is a beautiful experience; it's a precious gift. You are a precious gift.

If you feel that you didn't get to enjoy your childhood as an innocent child, there is no better time than the present to start playing. Playing heals. Playing breeds happiness. Playing is underrated as an adult. There is no time. It's silly. Adults don't deserve to play when they could be working, because it's good to be doing something that is productive. Ironically, PLAY is productive to our soul's evolution and true happiness. You get your body moving and your energy circulating. It feels good. You are allowed to both be an adult and play. Take that inner child to the park and go down the slide if that's what they want to do. Jump on a trampoline. Go to a concert with your friends. Go camping and explore the awe and wonder of nature. Run into the ocean uninhibited and let go. Go have fun!

Most adults feel like life needs to be serious—overly serious. Connecting with your nonserious inner child can help life be a little more lighthearted—if you allow yourself to change your attitude and perspective. I am not perfect at this at all. The truth is, being an adult does come with some heavy life "stuff" that is not always "fun" to deal with and go through. The good news is we do have the power inside of ourselves to choose how we relate to what is going on, and the question is: Are you going to let the low parts of life hold your essence hostage and suck your soul dry, or are you going to do the work and get to know yourself?

It is not uncommon for people to operate from "victim mode."

"Oh, poor me—my life sucks, everyone else has an easy life, but I have to deal with THIS. Are you kidding me? I didn't sign up for this!"

And the favorite line of ALL time in victim mode:

"It's not fair!"

Been there, done that! And even now, I need to catch myself when I find that I'm going there; entering into the rabbit hole of victim mode is the opposite of what your "little you" would tell you to do, and that's the key.

When you find yourself heading into negative land, just stop—stop what you are doing, stop what you are thinking—take a breath, and then ask yourself what your inner child would tell you to do, and whatever it is, that's your truth, that's your joy. Kids are simple. Kids play, laugh, eat, sleep, play again, and they LOVE, wholeheartedly. That's still in you, it's still there, and it doesn't matter if you've been jaded or burned; your inner child is still there and still is powerful beyond measure. Tap into that energy and remember when you were a kid. You felt like you could do anything in life, you could be anything; that's the energy I want you to tap into to increase your happiness.

LESSONS I LEARNED FROM MY GRANDMA

Redirection breeds happiness, and it can take you a long way. When you feel like life is getting complicated, all you need to do is to get redirected just like kids do. When my son was two years old, I learned the art of redirection. My grandma had come over for dinner, and my son was crying because he wanted to have a cookie for dessert. I told him he needed to have fruit instead. (He had already had a piece of cake and some candy at a friend's birthday party, so he had met his sugar quota for the day.) As I went through my list of everything I could do to get him to stop crying, my grandma simply, quietly, and gently asked, "Sweetie boy, did you go to the zoo the other day?" Almost immediately, he lit up, and with tears still on his cheeks, he said, "Yes!" Then my grams proceeded to ask him a ton of questions about what animals he saw there. He was hooked; he was fully present in that conversation—cookie, shmookie! He was completely into telling his great-grandma about the zoo! This was such an incredible scene to witness with such learning opportunities, not just as a mom regarding how to help a two-year-old who is sad but also as a reminder of how we as adults have the power to get redirected or redirect ourselves when it's needed!

You might be wondering HOW? The key is having the ability to let go of what is not serving us. Staying in "upset mode" is the opposite of beneficial for us in mind, body, and soul. It's having the ability to forget what was disturbing your peace and find something else to talk about or do that lights you up, just like how talking about the zoo excited my son. The past is the past.

Holding on to something is only preventing you from being in the flow and letting life continue, so you can experience everything incredible that is waiting for you. Feel those feelings and take some time to process and reflect—see what you can learn from those emotions, but then tell the upset ones that they don't have much time to stay there and hang out because you have your life to live.

When in doubt, connect with your inner child as she has a lot of knowledge to share with you on how you can live a happy life. That inner child of yours is wise beyond her years; she has a lot to say, and we as adults have much to learn and be inspired by. Our inner child constantly reminds us how to have a happy life; we need to choose to listen and then act.

Lizzie is a perfect example of MAN*ifesting. She manifested her man when she put in the work to get back to herself. Lizzie was a very put-together (or so it seemed to the world), successful thirty-one-year-old working in finance when she reached out to me to start therapy. She had it all. She was independently wealthy, living in New York City, with a great social life. She was "living it up" on the outside, but inside, Lizzie felt empty, lonely, lost, completely unworthy, and incapable of love.

LIZZIE, THE CHAMELEON

Lizzie was The Chameleon, and for a good reason. Lizzie's childhood was not ideal, and it stole her identity away from herself and from the soul she was born as. She had an insecure attachment style due to her relationship with her father. That insecure attachment style showed up in all her relationships (because our attachment styles always do). Lizzie's love from her father was conditional. He was unreliable and unpredictable; therefore, she had trouble trusting guys, never knowing if they would be there for her. She felt rejected by her father; consequently, she was always fearful of being rejected by men. Lizzie's father had a rough childhood, as his father left at an early age and would pop in unannounced once in a while. His mother was too busy working to care for him and his brother. There was no one to make him feel loved. His resentment and anger toward his father and his upbringing unconsciously carried into his parenting, which was subpar.

The only time Lizzie's father was loving toward her was when she got straight A's or did something with him that he liked to do, like fishing or going to a baseball game (both activities were not quite Lizzie's cup of tea). She felt like she could never do anything that entirely held up to his expectations except when she was being "perfect," but even then, she could feel that his love was not authentic. If Lizzie didn't meet her father's expectations, he would ignore her for a long time, leaving Lizzie feeling rejected again.

Because of her toxic relationship with her father, Lizzie would go to great lengths to be the woman whom the guys she dated were looking for, which was not who she truly was. Lizzie was The Chameleon, changing her colors in the name of love, constantly altering who she was or what she liked in order to be accepted by the man she wanted to love her (at the time).

As we know, all this pretending will only end in heartache. Not to mention, pretending takes so much effort. It's a lot easier just to be yourself, but Lizzie (and many others out there) needed to learn that for herself.

Lizzie's past boyfriends were all different, and she would mold herself into the shape of each one no matter what it cost her. Jack liked indie rock, so Lizzie did too. She stopped listening to her favorite, which was pop rock. Peter was a homebody, so Lizzie pretended to be an introvert who didn't enjoy going out all the time and being social (that could not be further from the truth). Instead, Lizzie would spend a lot of time in the kitchen, whipping up gourmet meals for Peter (she hated cooking). They could spend a weekend couch surfing, during which Lizzie was bored out of her mind, but she didn't want Peter to know. Gregg was uber-religious and enjoyed going to church every Sunday, so Lizzie would wake up early (which she hated to do), get all dolled up, and accompany Gregg to church, where she appeared to be cheery and ready to pray like the good Catholic girl that she was (or was she?). She was Christian! But for Gregg, Lizzie was Catholic.

Losing her religion is where she started to draw the line. Pretending to be Catholic was when she got fed up with herself and her behavior. She was tired, physically and emotionally. Lizzie was a night person, so waking up early every Sunday didn't do it for her. She knew she had to stop this cycle. After Gregg, she vowed that no man was going to dictate how she lived her life, and that's when she realized she didn't know how to do that herself. It was time to start therapy, dig deep, find out who she was, and know it in her bones so she could break free from being The Chameleon.

Lizzie came into her first session to work through the child-hood trauma that prevented her from finding her "person." Lizzie was very emotional and raw the minute she sat on the couch. (This is very common because people have often held in their thoughts and feelings for so long that it's a big cathar-sis to vent and get everything out.) Lizzie was devastated that she hadn't found her man yet. She felt like she was doing every-thing possible—on the apps, going to events, and saying yes to fix-ups—but even with all her dating, she had an energetic block inside.

Lizzie had forgotten who she was at her core, as the woman showing up on dates was an insecure, unsure, negative version of herself. Alongside her conditional-loving dad, she also shared with me that she grew up with a mom who would comment on her weight and a grandma who told her she would never find a man to marry. The boys at school would call her names; bullying was something Lizzie was not unfamiliar with. It makes sense why Lizzie showed up as a Chameleon date after date and in life day after day.

She wasn't aware of how much her childhood affected her adult life. She felt that that was then and this is now. She was "over it," she said. "The past was in the past." But that couldn't be further from the truth. The past was living in her consciousness 24/7. Yes, she managed to be very successful at work because, let's be honest, you work hard like Lizzie, and you will be suc-cessful. It was her dating life that was in shambles.

"If only I could be as confident in dating as I am in the boardroom," Lizzie pleaded through her tears.

Lizzie was confident in some areas of her life—at her job, with her friends, at yoga class—but not when it came to love, not when it came to opening her heart and being vulnerable. It took her a few sessions to realize that she was always conforming to every guy she met to try and impress him. She feared if she showed up as herself, the guy would leave, which always ended up happening anyway because every guy would eventually pick up on her inauthentic energy. Her Chameleon ways and lack of confidence became unattractive to them, so her fear became a self-fulfilling prophecy. It was a vicious cycle she was ready to end.

"I can't…I just can't do it anymore," Lizzie exclaimed. "I'm exhausted from trying to be someone I'm not. I'm effed up, and it's all my dad's fault for treating me horribly, and he still does. At least my mom stopped being unkind."

Lizzie was willing to shed her Chameleon skin, and she was prepared to do the work needed to find her man, The One she was meant to be with. But first, we had to address the culmina tion of negative energy. Lizzie would need to heal her relationship with her father—or at least forgive him—because the energy she held inside created her model of what a man is. We had to shift that energy into a more positive one for her to MAN*ifest her man, one who was nothing like her absent father.

The second issue was that Lizzie was in "victim mode." If you identify as a victim, then The Universe will continue to bring you experiences and relationships that validate that you're a victim, which is exactly what happened in Lizzie's love life.

Life happens for us, not to us. I needed Lizzie to know this because having that knowledge helps one shift out of "victim mode" into "thriving mode." Everything that happens in life is an opportunity for growth, upliftment, and more education about ourselves. There are beautiful nuggets of wisdom and beautiful gifts that can come from negative experiences; you just need to be open to seeing them and receiving them.

She understood that healing her relationship with her father wouldn't happen overnight, but she was willing to put in the work. She started to have compassion for her father, which allowed her to see that he was doing the best he could with the tools that he had (not a lot) and that he was limited in his ability to change because he wasn't self-aware enough to own up and take responsibility for his actions. While Lizzie couldn't fix her dad or take back his behavior, here was a chance for Lizzie to practice radical acceptance.

Radical acceptance is a concept I teach my clients that results in significant shifts and healing. Side note: acceptance is the first law of spirituality, meaning that if you can master it, you're pretty much set for life. Is radical acceptance easy? No, but does it free you and heal you? YES! I explained to Lizzie that with radical acceptance, it doesn't mean that you like how someone treated you or a particular situation; it means that you accept it with no judgment, and you trust that there's a reason why this relationship/experience has been brought into your life. Radical acceptance is you saying to The Universe, "OK, I see you, I get it. You gifted this relationship for me to learn how to love myself even more, regardless of what's happening in my outside world."

"I'm tired of wishing that I had a different dad and wishing that my dad would change. He's not going to. I know that it's up to me to change how I respond to him, and it's up to me to choose whether or not to engage with him as much as I do. And when he is not always the nicest man in the world, it's up to me to get triggered or not."

"Wait, what!? Lizzie, what did you just say? Was that really you saying that? Lizzie—you've learned!"

Our circumstances can teach us how to love ourselves fully because when we love ourselves unconditionally, rather than conditionally, we can show up as who we inherently are.

"Lizzie—you are right on track!" I said.

I was beaming with happiness for her. Witnessing someone transform is quite magical. When something finally clicks with a client, I get a little choked up because I can see the relief on their face, and their whole energy shifts. Watching a client release what doesn't serve them anymore is incredibly uplifting.

Through watery eyes, I continued, "So, how are you going to get to know yourself and love yourself more?" (Which brings me to her second issue of being in "victim mode.")

"Well, I'm not going to be a victim of my circumstances any-more. I'm going to accept my father the way he is, and when he treats me poorly, I'm just going to love myself more and know that how he is trying to make me feel is not the truth of who I am. When I get triggered by him or anyone, instead of going to my old negative narratives, I will remind myself of my worth, I'm going to remind myself of how lovable I am, and I will remind myself that I deserve love. I know that my dad is a victim of his childhood, but I don't need to let his behavior toward me dictate and predict my present and future. His past can keep him in the past, but I'm breaking free, and I'm going to set some major boundaries—this is my life, and I only have one life to live, and I'm not getting any younger."

Side note: *You can set "spiritual boundaries" with someone. You don't have to announce that you are setting a boundary. Telling* *someone that you are setting boundaries with them could exacerbate the problems because when you're dealing with someone who doesn't own up, telling them you are setting a boundary won't matter; they will be defensive and angry.*

MY CHAMELEON STORY

I was The Chameleon at one point, and I was utterly clueless about it. I wasn't conscious and self-aware enough to realize I was changing myself to fit each man's preferences. It's as if I (my authentic self) was sleeping, and my ego (my fear-based-mind-self) had taken over right before my eyes.

I met Brett at a deli in Los Angeles circa 2004. I was having brunch with my friend Jennifer, and he was sitting at the table right in front of us. The funny thing is that if I didn't have a bladder the size of a pea, I might not have met him and could have saved myself a few years with the wrong man. But as you've learned, and I finally learned, it couldn't have happened any other way because I was meant to have that relationship. That relationship held learning opportunities for me.

So, back to my pea-sized bladder. If I hadn't gotten up to go to the bathroom in the middle of the meal, I never would have noticed Brett. Sitting at the table, his back was to me, but on my way back from the bathroom, I couldn't help but notice his attractive face, wire-framed adorable glasses, and shaggy brown hair. I just had to say something to him.

Back at our table, Jennifer turned around and tapped him on his back—they sat back to back—and he turned around, which is when I proceeded to make up some lie about how I thought he looked familiar...yada, yada, yada. Jennifer ended up knowing him from the real estate field, always a small world. I, however, had never seen the boy in my life. Through small talk, I learned that he was a few years younger than me, which up until then was a problem for me, but I was getting "older" (twenty-eight), so I wanted to be more open to dating younger guys. Brett and I exchanged numbers, and I was excited to rob the cradle. OK, he wasn't that much younger—he was about to be twenty-five!

As I got to know him, I enjoyed spending time with him. Brett was fun, lots of fun. I had just come off a relationship with a guy who was the opposite of fun, and I welcomed the breath of fresh air that was Brett. Did I mention that he was fun? Well, I learned later on that was the only thing he was (to me). There was no real depth to the relationship, yet I remained drawn to him, so I wanted to be with him. He brought the fun. He was spontaneous, and although he was immature in many ways, his French mother had made certain that he was cultured. Sometimes I felt like I was dating a Frenchman who was different and sexy. He was also a bit of a game player and wasn't incredibly emotionally intelligent, which left me guessing how he felt about me sometimes. Since I wasn't the best communicator, I became The Chameleon instead of asserting myself, my needs, and my desires because of the fear that this intriguing "Frenchman" would disappear.

Brett loved to scuba dive. I, on the other hand, had never thought twice about partaking in the sport because (a) I'm the type of girl that likes to stay on land and get a tan at the beach, not go deep-sea diving and (b) when I was a little girl, my mom told me she knew someone who died from scuba diving, so it was always a "no gracias" for me. When Brett asked if I wanted to go scuba diving with him, I responded, "Yes, so fun!" when

I was thinking, *Hell, no! I have zero desire...please let's do something else, anything else...OK, maybe not anything else, definitely not skydiving either.* You get my point. My fear-based ego self (my mind) was answering, "Hell yes!" when my authentic self was saying, "No, thank you." Still, I proceeded to pay a lot of money to go to a month's worth of scuba classes to get certified to go scuba diving.

What the real f**k, Jaime!?

Brett came with my class and me to Catalina Island for our certification weekend, where he and I scuba-dived together. I have to say that being underwater was quite peaceful, but I was cold, the wetsuit was uncomfortable, and I was terrified the entire time of DYING! Was it an experience? Yes. Will I ever do it again? No! But the payoff for changing my colors was that I got to spend a weekend away with Brett. We went on dates, shared a waffle cone of ice cream, had great sex, and then the weekend was over.

Brett was also a big drinker, and I ended up drinking more than usual in that relationship. Spending money on things I didn't want and drinking too much—two red flags for me right there. There were more, but I wanted him to love me, and I feared that he would dump me if I made any move that wasn't to his liking. When we eventually broke up, I was angry that I had spent so much time and money on something that compromised my integrity. I was angry that instead of being honest with him, I had pretended to be someone I was not. Of course, I'm fun and adventurous, but my definition and his are pretty different. I wanted him to think I was fun and adventurous, and I didn't want to miss an opportunity to see him. This sounds so desperate.

Twenty-eight-year-old Jaime had so much learning to do, and I did learn my lesson because, after that relationship, I made a vow that I was never going to try to be someone I'm not. If a guy didn't like me for who I was, he wasn't the right guy for me. I was done being The Chameleon.

I'm sure you're wondering how Lizzie ultimately met her man. I left you hanging! The moment Lizzie became willing to heal her relationship with her father was the moment everything in her life began to change for the better. The Universe was rewarding her for her work. Classier and more mature men were showing up on her dating apps, and everywhere she went. The more she acted and felt like her authentic self, the more she met guys left and right—at the gym, coffee shop, Central Park, you name it. But the place where she ended up meeting The One was somewhere she had been all along. As much as she felt confident at work, she still wouldn't allow herself to shine in front of any man she thought could be a potential mate.

At work, in the past, Lizzie's blinders were on. She didn't want to be seen, and when she was seen, she would shrink. Her unresolved issues weren't allowing her to see what was right in front of her—a man who was everything she was looking for but believed he was so out of her league that she never entertained it.

Garrett had felt the same way about Lizzie, but when they were placed on a project together (thank you, Universe) that required them to travel to Philadelphia for a few days, the two got to know each other throughout the trip. Lizzie showed up as herself, and Garrett liked her for everything that she was. He loved that she was obsessed with comic books, cats, and folk music. What Lizzie considered quirky or "weird" was now something she was comfortable sharing with him—he stuck around, and they began dating.

Two years into their relationship, Garrett took Lizzie on a surprise trip to Comic-Con and proposed there, right in front of *Archie*, her favorite comic book exhibit. During his proposal, he slipped in that she is "the Veronica to his Archie." OK, kinda cheesy to you or me, but Lizzie ate it up because she was in love, and there wasn't a doubt in her mind that Garrett was her soul-mate. I still get updates from Lizzie once in a while, and even though she married Garrett years ago, she always tells me that she falls more in love with him yearly. Now, that's true love, and that's why I do this work. Lizzie had a lot of work to do, but it was all worth it. You will never regret investing in yourself. That's exactly what Lizzie did, what my clients do, and what I do too!

CHAPTER TWO EXERCISE: BE YOU

The purpose of this exercise is to assist you in remembering who you are. This exercise will help you access your authentic self, the self with the big S—your soul—the person you came as into this world before life, experiences, and negative relationships got in the way.

#1: Take out your MAN*ifesting journal. Make a list of all the positive qualities that make you "you." If you have trouble putting together the list, ask yourself how a family member or your best friend would describe you.

#2: Take your time and come up with at least ten items for your list. You can ask yourself these questions:

Who am I? What are my talents? What do I have to offer a relationship?

For example:

"I am witty."
"I am smart."
"I am attractive."
"I am silly."
"I am thoughtful."
"I am empathetic."
"I am a go-getter."
"I am creative."
"I am tenacious."
"I am loving."

Be as honest as possible; this is about being confident in who you are. I believe you can know the truth about how amazing you are while remaining modest and humble! It's all about being "self-full," not selfish! You are working on feeling whole and fulfilled, not full of yourself.

#3: Look at this list every night before you go to sleep; leave it on your nightstand. You can even make this list your screensaver on your phone. Close your eyes and set an intention that this list will integrate into your consciousness in your sleep state. Ask The Universe to merge the current you with the real you.

You are asking that you become more connected with yourself in service to being able to deeply connect with your "person" when he arrives. Let this be a reminder of who you genuinely are. Integrate within to remind you that you are your true authentic self. You must show up in life as your authentic self to manifest your person, The One who will be completely aligned with you and who will love you for ALL that you are, and you will do the same for him!

#4: This is also a time to ask for anything you desire. There's something magical that happens in our sleep state. Nothing is off-limits because the truth is that this world is abundant and anything is possible, so ask away. Remember that The Universe will always bring you what you need, not necessarily what you want, so always trust in that knowledge.

CHAPTER THREE

Set an Intention and Manifest All You Need

Affirmation: I am clear on who I am, what I am looking for, and what I deserve. I am a conduit for my heartfelt dreams so that The Universe can deliver all that is in alignment with my desires.

MANIFESTATION AND INTENTIONS ARE all about openness. Open your heart, open your mind, treat The Universe with the reverence and wonder it deserves, and The Universe will revere you and be wonderful right back. A crucial aspect of MAN*ifesting is setting your intention, but you can't just throw something out there and expect it to work. For instance, if you say to The Universe, "Please, just bring me a man, drop him on my doorstep. I'm ready. Let's get this party started," The Universe has no idea what to do with that!

Anything in life that is worth manifesting is worth putting in the work to get clear on exactly what it is you desire to manifest. If you were looking for a new job, would you pray to The Universe and simply ask for a job, or would you be specific and ask for a job that you were passionate about in a field that you were great at, and perhaps in a location that suited you? You might even ask for a nice boss, flexible hours, and chummy office mates. See where I'm going with this? Telling The Universe to find your man is not going to do it. Setting your intentions and being open to The Universe bringing you "this or something better for the highest good of all concerned" is the way!

To MAN*ifest, you need to get crystal clear on what you're looking for, and then you need to imagine your life with your man already in it. Up until now, have you sat down to think about, in-depth, the qualities that you would like your man to have? This is beyond important. Many women are more often than not walking around blindly looking for love, a lot like a chicken with its head cut off. We think we know what we want, but by doing this work, we soon discover that what we want is either out of date or that we never ever sat down to think about what is most important to us. If you aren't clear about your desires, then The Universe will not be specific and will deliver a man who isn't aligned with you, and we already know how that goes! It's what you lived in the past, and I'm guessing it didn't quite work out the way you wanted it to. It's time to clear up your intentions.

As you start to get clear on what you're looking for, it's important to remember that The Universe will bring you what you need, which is not necessarily what you want. Can you trust in that? As humans, we think we know what we need, but ultimately, in the giving over and letting go, you will see that the man for you will be even better than you could have imagined— if you trust the process and let go of control.

I can't tell you how many times a client comes into my office with tears rolling down her face, feeling beyond frustrated.

"I feel like I am doing everything to manifest love, and nothing is working," she says. "What am I doing wrong?"

She isn't doing anything wrong per se, which is what I explain, but she just hasn't learned the art of MAN*infesting. It is an art, and it does take practice. There is a lot to learn, but once you have it down, learning how to get clear on what you are looking for is a game changer and MAN*ifesting becomes a piece of cake. Instead of a random man showing up next, you will find that even if your next boyfriend isn't The One, he will at least be closer to it than any man who came before. The relationship will feel different, because you will know that you're on track.

THE NONNEGOTIABLES

The first rule of MAN*ifesting is that you must cut your list of a thousand "it'd be nice if" items to three to five nonnegotiables. If your list is too long, it is too chaotic and too unorganized for The Universe, and things will get lost in translation, resulting in the wrong man for you—again. But how do you come up with this short list? Take some time and think about what really matters to you. What qualities do you need your "person" to have? Choose positive attributes like "trustworthy," not the negative version: "I need a man who doesn't lie." Every woman will have a different list because every woman is unique. What you are looking for in your man will not be what your BFF is looking for. There might be some overlap, but not every nonnegotiable will be shared. I believe that we base our nonnegotiables on either positive childhood relationships or things that we have learned from past adult romantic relationships.

Do some soul-searching and imagine your everyday life with this man. What are the musts? Religion and political views can be included, because they tend to play a huge part in relationships and can cause major issues if two people aren't aligned or they judge each other for their beliefs or views.

An example of a nonnegotiable list that I like to share, whether in a session with a client, on my show, or a podcast, comes in the form of an acronym. CERT, so you can be "certain" that you will manifest your match. *C* is for comfort. You want to feel comfortable with your man. You want to think that being with him brings you solace from the stresses of life at the end of the day. He feels like home. *E* is for empathy. You are empathetic, so you want to be with a man who will be able to be empathetic as well. When you share how you feel, he won't dismiss it; he will listen and do his best to understand. *R* is for respect. Women who don't respect themselves will manifest a man who doesn't respect them. Respect is huge. In a soulmate relationship, both parties respect one another. *T* is for trust. This one seems obvious, but it's beyond important. You need a man who is 100 percent trustworthy. If you have any doubt that he is not, he is not the right one for you. Trust is one of the most crucial building blocks for a relationship's solid foundation.

SET YOUR INTENTION, THEN SET IT FREE

Once you have your list, you have your intention—one that is extremely clear because you know what you are looking for—and once you set that intention free and put it out there, The

Universe also has a grasp on it. And the best part is, you don't need to constantly be thinking about how to get your man anymore. Know that after releasing your intention into The Universe, The Universe will always know what's in your heart so that you can relax a bit. You can be more present in your own life. Let The Universe do its work, and you go enjoy your dating journey with as little stress as possible. Remember, dating is supposed to be fun. You are allowed to have fun, you know.

But what if you've already done this work? What if you've gotten clear as a bell on the kind of man you desire and you've shared your short list ad nauseam with The Universe? What then?

Enter The Faultfinder, the woman who is subconsciously battling her man—and herself. This is yet another fear-based dating persona.

JOANNA, THE FAULTFINDER

"I swear, there is something wrong with every man I meet." My client Joanna was The Faultfinder. "I feel like G-d hates me. Why does he keep sending me these losers?"

Her ego was working overtime. On every first date, her ego would do everything to keep her safe. She would find fault in every guy she dated, rejecting them before they could reject her. She was so desperate not to feel the pain of rejection that she would go to great lengths to avoid getting hurt, which ultimately backfired—she always ended up getting hurt.

"Nothing ever works out for me," she told me. "This whole dating, love, relationship, and marriage thing sucks. I have run out of hope."

But every time, she'd dust herself off and get back out there, but not before putting on her armor to make certain that she was protected from making a real connection with a man. Joanna was unaware of this rinse-and-repeat cycle, completely clueless that she was the common denominator. So, I asked her for an example of an "unworthy" man.

"OK, well…there was this guy, Chris," she said. "I have to say that he was a smoke show, but I hated how he dressed…"

I waited for her to continue giving me all the other reasons he was to be thrown in the trash.

I waited…and waited.

"Was there a period at the end of that sentence?" I asked. "Or is there more?"

"No, that's it," Joanna said. "I went out with him a few times just to see if his clothes improved, but they didn't."

Joanna was so focused on his clothes that she didn't give the poor guy a fighting chance.

"Was he nice?"

"Yes!"

"You mentioned he was good looking."

"OMG, yes—uber hot!"

"Was he smart?"

"He is in finance," she said, pausing to think. "So, I'm guessing yes."

"What did you talk about?"

"I don't know. Lots of things here and there. The dates consisted of him asking me questions."

"Would you ask him questions back?"

"No."

"Why not?"

"I was too annoyed that he didn't know how to dress for a date."

"Joanna, how are you supposed to get to know him past his clothing if you don't ask him any questions?"

"I know, you're right. but I wasn't in the mood because I couldn't stand the clothes."

"So, you completely wrote him off because of what was going on, on the outside. There could be an incredible person in there! What was so bad about his clothes?"

"He wore a plaid shirt on the first date. On the second date, he wore sneakers instead of nicer shoes."

"Where did you go on that date?"

"We went to this charming, trendy pizza place."

"It was pizza," I gently reminded her.

"I know, but it was *trendy*!"

"And the third date?"

"Oh, don't get me started on the third date. He wore a brown belt with black shoes!"

Joanna came in week after week with more proof that she needed to heal her faultfinding ways. There was Todd, who didn't have a great relationship with his mom, so she wrote him off, even though she loved everything else about him top to bottom and inside out. Then there was Matt, who loved sports just a little too much for Joanna. She was worried that he wouldn't spend time with her, so she rejected him. Joe was a very successful businessman, but he didn't have a master's degree, so that wasn't good enough for Joanna. And finally, there was Daniel, whom she went on two dates with and had a phenomenal time. She said that he checked off everything on her list except for the fact that he lived in New Jersey and she lived in New York. It was too far for her. Excuses, excuses, excuses. Her ego (her mind) was trying to keep her safe, but all it was doing was keeping her further away from her "person."

By this point, my intuition was telling me loud and clear that this woman had been hurt and was terrified of getting hurt again. So I felt at this point it would be a good idea to investigate further and gather some data from Joanna's past relationships. My hunch was validated tenfold. I learned that Joanna had a few boyfriends in the past, and ultimately each one ended in Joanna feeling rejected and heartbroken. Instead of doing the healing work and learning how to love herself and know her worth, Joanna had gone the opposite direction and decided that she would never be rejected again. The excellent news for her is that she accomplished her goal. The bad news is that because she was The Faultfinder, no man could ever get past the first or second date.

I pointed out that her faultfinding may be a defense mechanism, something she was doing to keep her unhurt, but what it was doing instead was keeping her alone and further away from her intention—to manifest her "person." She couldn't possibly set her intention for what she was looking for in a man because she was too wrapped up in protecting herself. She needed to take her power back and get past her fears of imperfection to get clear on what she was looking for. Up until now, Joanna had no clue how detrimental her pickiness was to her life and no idea how her faultfinding ways hindered her from meeting her man, but when she had her ah-ha moment, it was like the brightest light turned on in her head. Joanna did one of the fastest and most astonishing 180s I have ever witnessed. She left her session that day as if she was walking on water.

If you haven't yet experienced this, being intentional in life and in love makes a ginormous difference. Once Joanna grasped the concept of intentions, she started to get excited about dating, and her anxious and protective energy transformed into hopeful energy. The week after, she came into my office with a massive smile.

"Jaime, everything has changed," she said, gleaming. "I challenged myself to be present on my next date. Just enjoy the moment and see my date for all that he was, not focus on any aspect that wasn't ideal, and IT WORKED!"

"That's amazing, Joanna. Tell me more!"

"OK, so this guy Tom showed up to the date, and I was immediately attracted to him. The conversation was flowing, and we were laughing and having fun. He was chivalrous and witty. He had amazing arms (I could tell when I hugged him initially), and I felt this energy between us. It was that energy that you always talk about, Jaime—the kind beyond chemistry! I was entirely in the moment and practicing being present, like you've taught me…until…Tom mentioned that he was overweight as a kid, and then a million thoughts rushed into my mind.

"'I'm going to fall in love with this man, and then he will die of a heart attack because he is going to be overweight again at some point. Our kids will be fat. What if all he wants to do when we retire is hop in the car and go for a ride to the drive-through at McDonald's?'"

"Wow, Joanna, your mind sure is creative."

"I know, believe me, it's not fun…or shall I say it used to not be fun having all that chaos and fear going on in my mind, but this time, with Tom, was different."

Joanna had taken everything she had been learning and put it into action. She allowed those thoughts to be there, but then she looked into her date's eyes and saw him for the human he is, and her fear disappeared. Instead of immediately judging his faults, she listened to his story, and as it turns out, looking at his humanness made her more attracted to him. He said that he hated being overweight so much that he vowed to change his lifestyle and never go back again, and he told Joanna that he wants to be around for as long as possible—for his future wife and kids.

"I was blown away by how my little shift made such a monumental difference in my experience on that date," she said.

"Exactly, Joanna. You see how The Universe rewards you when you make subtle shifts. The more shifts you make, the more you will evolve. It's a cumulative effect!"

Joanna needed to remind herself of her old faultfinding ways once in a while to snap herself out of it. By stepping out of fear mode into loving mode, she could relax into being more in the moment and seeing men for all that they are, not just the little things that bothered her in the past.

Joanna dated Tom for a few years. They even started a fitness business together, but ultimately realized that they were better as business partners and decided to break up amicably. It was so amicable that the two remained such great friends, and Joanna retains the confidence that The One is out there.

Every time I see Joanna, she begins the session with gratitude—gratitude for listening to her inner child, knowing that she shouldn't give up, shouldn't settle, and that there is more to learning how to MAN*ifest.

"Working with you is hands down the best investment I have ever made," she will say to me often as we find her way on her journey together.

I was Joanna's guide, there to help her navigate through those murky waters of her past to heal and emerge as the brilliant woman she is today, this woman who is so full of life and positive energy.

"I feel like I look and feel different," she recently said to me. "Younger even...does that sound crazy?"

"Not at all!" I said.

For when we heal and our energy shifts, we can appear different: a little "glowy-er." It's as if we can begin to age backward—or at least it feels and looks like it. When we stop seeking perfectionism within ourselves and in others, we make room for healing with peace in our hearts. When your mind, body, and soul are all in alignment, you can relax into the flow of your life. Indeed, living with less stress is proven to lead to a longer life.

When you have inner balance, things that happen in your outer world reflect that; it's the ultimate goal. I hope you are beginning to see how powerful this work is—and you're only on chapter 3. My little grasshoppers, you are on your way, and I'm delighted and honored to be here with you for the ride.

CHAPTER THREE EXERCISE: BE SELF-CONNECTED

As you've learned in this chapter, there is a fine line between knowing what you want and not being so broad in your requests that it confuses The Universe. There is a space between being so picky you'll only settle for impossible perfection and being so open that your desires get lost in translation. We want to land in the middle, with our sound list of what we want in The One. The exercise in this chapter is about first gathering internal information and then sharing it with The Universe.

#1: Close your eyes before you begin writing. Take a few moments in this quiet space. Closing the eyes can help you access the information that is within you but that might not be right on the surface. This is what you call a closed-eye/open-eye exercise, because some things will come to you when your eyes are open and others will arrive only after closing your eyes, and, obviously, you need to keep your eyes open to write.

*#2: Open your MAN*ifesting journal to a blank page to make a list of all the things you're looking for in your man—The One. Now, write down your list—anything at all that comes to your mind or heart. Don't worry how long or short your list is, and do not judge yourself for what you want to write down.*

#3: After you have made your list, now it's time to narrow the list to three to five nonnegotiables. Remember, these are the most important things you are looking for in The One. This is what your man must have to spend the rest of his life with you.

An example of a list of nonnegotiables:

Respectful
Motivated
He prioritizes me
Trustworthy

And another list:

Practices a religion/has faith in a higher power
Loves sports
Financially stable
He has an amazing sense of humor

#4: *Keep your list with you or memorize it. You will use this list as you continue on your MAN*ifesting journey. You will find that moving forward, when you're on dates and assessing your experience on dates, this list will help you to hone in on what is most important to you. If the guy seems promising, continue to see him. If you're not certain whether or not he has all of your nonnegotiables, keep on dating him until you know. If you can tell after the first date that he definitely does not complete your list, then you send blessings to him and move on.*

When I ask my clients to make their lists, I find that they feel strongly about certain things they were unaware of in the past, so being clear on their nonnegotiables truly helps them to MAN*ifest. It will help you too! Keep in mind that every woman's list will look different, and that's because all of you are different and unique.

You have your nonnegotiables, but don't throw away the rest of your list. We're going to use it in an upcoming chapter. You made that whole list for a reason, so just because we are not using it right now, it's not a waste of time. Everything I ask of you in this book—even your time reading it—is an investment in you. You are investing your time and energy into you, and I can promise that it will be the greatest investment you will ever make because finding love and having the honor of living the rest of your life with your soulmate is beyond priceless—life is richer, more fruitful, more meaningful, and way more fun!

CHAPTER FOUR

Letting Go of Laser Focus

Affirmation: "I release what I think should happen and trust that life will unfold in divine timing, the way it is supposed to unfold. I am in the flow of life, and I let go of trying to control it."

WHEN STEPHANIE WALKED INTO my office, the anxiety she exuded was palpable. She fidgeted on the couch, constantly twitching her foot, as she explained what brought her in. Stephanie had been dating Jason off and on for the past year and a half, and she was fed up with the way she was being treated by him. She had come to me looking for advice on how to get him to act the way she wanted.

Jason was an alcoholic who was unwilling to commit and often disappeared from Stephanie's life for days at a time, ignoring her repeated texts. He was cold and shut off by day, but at night (when he was drunk), he'd be sweet and lovey-dovey, talking about their future, telling her he loved her, and getting her hopes up. It was hard for Stephanie to know whether she could take him seriously.

But what finally drove Stephanie to therapy was that she was tired of always being the one to reach out to Jason, always the one to initiate plans. She told me that she wanted a man who stepped up, made plans, and always responded to her texts. She wanted a man who was there for her, whom she could rely on.

After she'd finished giving me the lowdown on her relationship, I asked her a question.

"Have you ever just waited for him to initiate or reach out to you?"

She paused to give it some thought, her leg still bouncing up and down.

"Well, no. I mean, I'll sometimes wait a few days, but then I will need to know whether we are meeting up at McFadden's, like we do every Wednesday, so I always end up texting him on Tuesday night or Wednesday morning."

"Do you think he feels like he doesn't need to reach out because he knows you'll eventually contact him?"

She looked down.

"Maybe," she said quietly, before starting up again with her spiel.

"But I can't just wait for him to text, because I need to know what he's doing and where he is. I mean, he can get into trouble sometimes if he drinks too much, so I want to know where he is and who he's with...so that I can know he's OK."

I nodded and took some notes. I could see how this was a frustrating relationship for Stephanie.

"Stephanie, I believe that a healthy relationship is one in which you can relax and feel at peace. Do you feel that way in your relationship with Jason?" I asked her.

She shrugged her shoulders.

Stephanie was the opposite of relaxed in this relationship. In fact, I can't count how many of her sessions and phone calls began with, "I have so much anxiety right now!" Instead of being at ease and comfortable in this relationship, she was fixated on keeping things going with Jason—no matter what! Her anxiety stemmed from her discomfort with the fact that she didn't know the outcome of their relationship. Stephanie spent a lot of her time and energy texting Jason.

While texting is a brilliant technology and has certainly made life easier in some facets of our lives, in the world of dating, texting is a minefield.

"Should I text back or wait a little longer? Ten minutes, a week, two weeks, a half-hour? HOW LONG SHOULD I WAIT TO TEXT HIM BACK? WHAT'S THE RIGHT ANSWER? GOD, GIVE ME THE RIGHT ANSWER! When I text him back, what should I text? Should I put in an emoji? A heart? No, that's too much. A smiley. Yes, the LOL smiley! Wait, what if he doesn't know what it means, and he thinks I'm crying because I'm sad, not laughing so hard that I'm crying? Or no emoji at all? Because what if he thinks I like him too much? But if I *don't* put an emoji, what if he thinks I'm boring and not fun?"

And it goes on and on and on. I know you've been there, so you get it!

Communicating through text is filled with the unknown. Think about the anxiety created by those pesky three dots, the ones that signify someone is responding, the ones that disappear with no explanation. "Did they stop? Are they mad? Did I turn them off? WHAT WERE THEY GOING TO SAY?" Or worse yet is when you get ghosted. Send a text and then stare at your phone for the next five hours...waiting, waiting, waiting...

for the response that never comes. When it comes to texting, not knowing the outcome (the unknown) drives us *crazy*, and that's an understatement.

Constant texting is a pattern that people can get trapped in now that we have the means to send a simple "what's up" or "what are you doing?" at any moment of every day. This is why when you're just starting to date someone, I encourage holding off on texts you write simply as an excuse to make contact with him. It signals boredom or neediness and tends to cause a guy to lose interest. Is there something important you need to ask him or tell him, e.g., there was an avalanche and you're making sure he wasn't buried alive or you need to let him know that your company is relocating you to Guam? Then sure, send an explicit text. Otherwise, let him have the opportunity to pursue you. Don't take that job away from him.

Texting wasn't the only troubling pattern of behavior Stephanie was exhibiting. The more Stephanie and I talked about the patterns she and Jason had established, the more it seemed clear that she was laser-focused on this relationship working out at all costs. Texting was just one way she had (perceived) control. I didn't understand the draw to Jason as it didn't seem like he was giving her ANYTHING that she needed. It became clear to me that Stephanie had convinced herself that Jason was The One, and she was going to do everything in her power to make it happen.

STEPHANIE, THE CONTROL FREAK

Stephanie was stuck in the dating persona of The Control Freak. When you are being The Control Freak in a relationship, it means you are obsessed with things working out, and you fixate on things needing to go a certain way, because this relationship *must* work out. But being The Control Freak is draining. Because, for starters, there is no such thing as control. Control is an illusion. Even so, trying to control a relationship often pushes men away.

Men like freedom, and they like to be the one in the driver's seat. Now, I'm not saying that you need to be subservient to a man. Hell no! It is the twenty-first century, and you deserve to have a say in things just as much as your man. But men do not respond well to the energy of a woman who is relentlessly pushing things in one direction or another. This is the reason that Jason wouldn't respond to Stephanie's texts. Stephanie was The Control Freak, and Jason knew she'd always be there—she wanted the relationship to work. He didn't need to do much. In fact, he knew that she would come back to him, regardless of what he did or didn't do. Her neediness was now driving him away.

Once I could clearly see the destructive relationship pattern they had gotten into, I gave Stephanie a challenge.

"I want you to feel what it would be like to be free from your need to control Jason or know where he is at all times," I said. "I am challenging you to only *respond* to his texts this week. Let him be the one to initiate. Do not text Jason."

She looked at me as if I'd just asked her to climb Mount Everest, with no shoes, no food, and with a blindfold on, but she did commit to the challenge.

The week in between Stephanie's sessions was pretty much crickets, which was unusual for her. Normally, I get an email or twelve with "updates" and "emergencies." Apparently, her MIA-ness wasn't a sign that things were going well with her "no texting rule." She was MIA because she was busy at work and busy texting Jason.

"I'm sorry, but I couldn't do it," she said, storming into her next appointment.

And then began the excuses—why she *had* to text, *had* to call, and *had* to stop by! Every week it was the same. She'd be sharing her plan for how to get Jason to do what she wanted, and I'd be thinking: *Please don't text him. I know how this ends, and it's not pretty.* But there's only so much you can do with a client. I, too, cannot control anyone's behavior. Controlling people is not my job. What I *can* do is suggest modifications that might produce a different result; however, it's the client who has to be the one frustrated by the same outcome—over and over and over again to make a change.

Therapists want to save their clients from heartache just as parents want to save their children from pain, but we know that everyone needs to make their own mistakes on their journey as we grow and evolve and become stronger and wiser. A changed outcome doesn't happen overnight, but it can happen sooner rather than later if the client is willing to do the work. In the meantime, it can be disheartening to watch the repetition. I knew that eventually one day Stephanie would get fed up enough that she would be ready to make a change.

"What would you accomplish by texting him?"

I can't tell you how many times I asked her that in our sessions, and she always had an answer, a reason, an excuse.

"If I don't text him, he'll forget about me." This is the "lack mentality." The truth is that if that happened then she would know that the relationship just wasn't meant to be, but Stephanie was not there yet.

One of the problems that Stephanie was dealing with was the fact that she didn't think about the consequences of her actions.

Her need to manage the relationship and know where Jason was at all times became more powerful than thinking about what her behavior (and addiction to texting) might be creating. Her need to know was more important than her need to be treated right—the folly of The Control Freak.

Stephanie would need to love and respect herself before a man was going to do the same. She had to release her laser focus on their future and find her flow if she was going to be able to admit to where they were right now.

THE ART OF FLOW

We've been told a billion times since childhood to FOCUS! The importance of paying attention to the task at hand is drilled into us, so it's no surprise that when it comes to finding our forever love, we rely on the same method. FOCUS! In our search for love, we believe our single-minded, willful determination to *make* it happen will make it happen. But, when it comes to love and The Universe, *where* you focus your attention matters more than the focus itself.

What we focus on is what The Universe brings to us, therefore a healthy focus is a balanced focus. Here's how that balance works. When you go overboard on wanting someone or something, the power you give to the fear of *not* having whom or what you want becomes greater than your dream of what you desire. Instead of what you desire, The Universe picks up on this stronger signal of fear and gives you what you are focusing on the most—which is the *not having*.

Ramaa Krishnan, one of my spiritual teachers, pointed out something quite interesting when she was teaching this concept.

It is something that happens to all of us at some point, yet, until we become conscious and aware of it, it can lead to an undesired outcome. She said that when you start dating a man, you are feeling all the feels; you are excited about him, you start imagining your life together—the white picket fence, you see it all. The problem is that the moment the heavenly feelings are born, so is the idea that you are terrified that the relationship will end. Even though you spend a lot of time in "heaven land," you are also residing in "fear land" and the fear of the relationship ending is ever more present than the enjoyment of the relationship and trusting that things will be OK. There is an underlying beneath-the-surface current of fear that hangs out ALL. THE. TIME. Because of this constant current of fear, The Universe arranges for the relationship to end because that's what you had been focusing on. Do your best to be conscious of what you are focusing on. Choose to focus on love and trust, not fear and doubt.

The Universe wants us to trust it. It wants us to come to it with open hands, not a death grip. The Universe responds to you trusting it. Laser focus or fixation will backfire.

Women tend to be planners by nature. But when it comes to love, I've learned that the less you plan and desperately hold on to a desired outcome and the more you tap into the flow of The Universe, the sooner The One will show up. Do your best to not have an attachment to the outcome and you will allow the flow of life.

Flow is the state of being that asks us to trust The Universe and lean into the current of life. Just like a powerful river rushing downstream, life is in a state of flow. It knows where it is going, when you'll meet your man, and how you'll meet him. The Universe wants us to trust its direction, relax, and enjoy the ride.

But we often choose a state of resistance, and we fight the current. Being in resistance versus acceptance will get you nowhere.

Stephanie's perfect guy was downstream, but because of her laser focus on Jason, she was swimming upstream, exhausted, grabbing at any flimsy branch on the bank, desperately hanging on to get the outcome she wanted. But it wasn't happening, and she couldn't get into the flow until she trusted that all would unfold the way it was meant to.

As I sat there listening to Stephanie fight with The Universe, it reminded me of the time I finally had my own breakthrough and let go of control.

I, like Stephanie, had wasted a lot of years convinced that a certain guy was The One. His name was Ben. (I share our entire five-year "saga" in chapter 7, "The One Before The One.") Ben was the guy I was convinced I was going to marry before I met The One who was the *real* guy I was going to marry. Many of us have a One before The One.

When it became clear that things were not going to work out with Ben, I threw myself into dating again and got myself into The Control Freak pattern with Josh. It was evident after a few dates that Josh and I weren't right for each other. It didn't take long before we stopped going on real dates and instead sent each other booty calls. I needed more and knew in my gut that Josh wasn't The One, but my mind loved tricking me into thinking that he *could* be, because of our off-the-charts addictive chemistry.

One Sunday morning, I was driving from the city to my weekly Sunday brunch at my grandparents' house in the burbs. Over lox and bagels, my grandma Esther usually acted as my therapist while my grandpa Jack kindly listened (or pretended to, as his hearing aids weren't always turned on), interjecting once in a while to update us on how the Cubs were playing.

I had been up late (or early, as some might say) the night before with Josh. After the nights we spent together, I always woke up feeling empty, lonely, and sad. Yet somehow, I kept on convincing myself that "this time" would be different. "This time" we'd connect over real things instead of just having sex and eating late-night pizza. I wanted to force this thing that wasn't right into being the right thing. I was not in touch with my intuition (enough) at that point. I was so scared that I'd never have a connection with someone like I did with Ben, so even if things didn't feel amazing and I knew it was a detrimental relationship, I still held hope that "this time" it could turn into something real.

Ah, the lie of "this time." We waste a lot of time on men who aren't right, buying into the lie that "this time it will be different."

It never is.

I was in such a bad mood that day heading to my grand-parents that even the beautiful weather couldn't take me out of my misery. Listening to an array of my favorite depressing love songs, I sank deeper into victim mode. Tears poured out of my eyes. When I glanced at myself in the rearview mirror, it was a pretty ugly scene. The mascara I had on from the night before was running in black streaks all down my face. My eyes were red, and there was nothing wild or appealing about my bedhead.

I started to try to shake off my sad feelings before I got to brunch by doing some positive self-talking, which would work from time to time. I told myself that life goes on, and I should be feeling better in no time. But this time, something was different when I said that to myself because it made me more depressed. I thought, *Yes, life goes on, but why isn't it taking me with it??* In that moment I was in major "victim mode" comparing myself to everyone else who had been lucky enough to move on with their lives, get married, and start families. I was left behind and life was not taking me with it. I was beyond sad and knew I had to make a change in order for my life to shift and *take me with it.*

I was done—done with feeling (and looking) horrible after meaningless nights with Josh. When I'm feeling down, I listen to love songs because they make me cry and feel worse because why not cry and feel worse—it's fun...right? I tuned into SiriusXM's love station, and the song "Endless Love" was playing. Normally in this situation, I would've continued to bawl my eyes out, but this was different. My pathetic tears turned into hopeful tears. Somehow I shifted from lonely mode to hopeful mode. I was inspired and empowered all at once. I wanted an "Endless Love" relationship, and it was in that moment that I knew that I was back on track. I reminded myself of my worth and reminded myself that that's exactly what I deserve.

Something about the air blowing through my hair and the empty road ahead of me made me realize that I needed to stop doing things the way I'd been doing them. I declared that I was no longer going to give in to the booty call. I was no longer going to give in to anything that lacked meaning—never, ever again. I felt strong, and for the first time, instead of getting mad at myself for all the mistakes I had made, I felt an abundance of compassion for that Jaime who kept making mistake after mistake, never learning, never moving, and, most importantly, who hadn't been growing and thriving.

I needed to trust that down this road of life was my happily ever after. I didn't know when it would come. I didn't know what it would look like. But I knew it was there. I was headed in the right direction. I just needed to surrender to that truth and enjoy the damn ride.

That day, along with the booty calls and the meaningless relationships, I declared that I was done driving the bus. I needed to find a different driver, because I was exhausted and clearly not the skilled navigator that I thought I was. It was time to let go and let *guide*; I had to completely trust that if I took my foot off the pedal, everything would still work out.

When I arrived at Esther and Jack's house full of energy, bursting through the door proclaiming, "I'm free! Free at last!" you can imagine the expression of pure "WTF-ness" on their sweet faces.

Grams excitedly uttered, "Congratulations, Jaime Girl, but what are you free from?"

"Grams and Gramps, I'm free from my past. I'm free from my need to control, and I'm free from any man *ever* making me feel anything less than wonderful."

At the table, amid a spread meant for three but robust enough to feed seventy, I tried my best to explain my epiphany. Thinking I'd gone a little cray-cray, Grams kept feeding me bagels. Yes, I was going crazy, but yes, *it was beautiful*. I somehow managed to wipe the scary mascara off my face, and all Grams did was take me in and hold me tight in probably one of the most loving hugs I've ever received from her. I believe it was because she was, in that moment, sharing her intense love and knew that I was going to eventually get to this point, but no one, not even her love, could have gotten me there—I needed to reach my clarity and my "aha" moment, my "knowing my worth moment," on my own. She is an angel on earth. We cried together as I released my past. Being held by her reassured me that I was physically held and also figuratively held and supported by The Universe. The love and the worth that she always saw in me and how she looked at me were finally how I started looking at myself, as a woman who was pure love just like her. I was poised on the threshold of my new experiment.

From that day forward, I made it a point to get out of my own way. I began to trust that The Universe would bring the right man at the right time. I was done wasting time with men who were wrong for me. I was done being in control. All that had done was distract me from being open to "Mr. Right," and I was done with "Mr. Right Now" for good. Instead of gripping so tightly to finding my person, I was going to let go and trust that if it was meant to be, it would happen. The Universe didn't need my manipulations. In fact, those manipulations and the desire for control were blocking everything I truly wanted.

Over the next few weeks, I experienced tiny slipups when I tried to control what was going to happen next with a guy instead of being present, but each time I forgave myself, chose to be kind, and returned to the groove of surrender and flow. Soon, I started having a ton more fun with my friends and being more present in my everyday life—instead of being fixated on the future or living with regret about the past. Sure enough, toward the end of that summer, I had my first delicious date with my now husband, Bryan. Two and a half years later at our wedding, our first dance was to "Endless Love," *and* those words are engraved inside both of our wedding rings. I'd say that was a full "circle" story, pun intended.

FIND YOUR FREEDOM

We think we're doing everything to MAN*ifest our man, but the truth is, wanting something or someone with too much of a tight grip hinders our ability to make it happen. Controlling the "when" and "how" of our "who" isn't our job—it's The Universe's job.

Past the chatter in our mind that bombards us day and night, past our own laser focus, is a place of openness where we can receive the messages, insights, *and the man* we desire. Trusting in The Universe helps us kick back. So, you see, there is a self-fulfilling prophecy to all of this. Worry that it will never happen, and it will never happen. Relax and know it's on its way, and the doorbell rings and it all begins.

Surrendering to the notion that The Universe has already picked out an incredible guy for you gives you the confidence to be in the flow and to stop comparing where you are right now with where "everyone else" seems to be.

However, this knowing does not give you permission to sit on your tushy and wait for your amazing life to begin, but it does allow you to stop kicking yourself for every situation that doesn't turn out the way you had it planned. Trusting and surrendering allows you to feel a hundred pounds lighter and allows light to flow through and around you. Your knowing will be your buoy during the days or moments you are tempted to sink into the past or into your story of "I'm not worthy."

You came to this book because you are in the dating game, and you've had some good times and some that weren't so good (OK, mortifying and disastrous is more like it—I've been there, too, honey). Our hearts are here, *all in*, ready, willing, and eager, but unless we pause the frenzied beating of our pulse for a moment to pick up the signs The Universe is sending, we remain naïve in believing we are in control.

We are not in control. We need to let go and let ourselves be guided.

If life is a journey, I'm asking you to now stop at this sign and hear this: life happens *for* you not *to* you. Everything that happens in life is all for our learning, growth, and upliftment. We all go through phases of losing ourselves or feeling lost, but The Universe loves and supports us, and it can keep us on track if we allow it to do so.

To surrender is not an act of weakness. *Au contraire.* Surrendering is a supreme act of strength. When I'm running on empty or uncharacteristically obsessing over something I cannot control, I remind myself that obsessing or worrying is a waste of time.

I know you may be saying, "Jaime, come on. How can I stop worrying about never finding someone? How can I *not* obsess over a new guy who I'm really excited about?"

You can most definitely get excited about a new prospect. You can imagine a future with him and think about the next steps on the journey, but you need to catch yourself before getting attached to the outcome. Flow requires the letting go, the open arms, the trust that what is supposed to be will be. Obsession is laser-focused, fixated. Worrying (anxiety) is future focused. Wallowing (depression) is focused too much on the past. You can dream, you can pray, you can imagine...as long as you let go of those pictures and know that if it isn't this guy, someone even better will come along.

When you feel yourself getting too focused, you can repeat this mantra: *I trust that The Universe will bring me this or something better for the highest good of all concerned.*

We *think* we know what is best for us, but we don't. The Universe will deliver what is most aligned with us; it's just a matter of cultivating the patience that is needed while waiting for your man to arrive.

When I start ruminating in the future-based "what if" zone, I will say out loud (or to myself if I'm in line at Starbucks), "Bring it back now. Come back to the present," so that I can reconnect to this moment and trust that everything will work out to end up the way it is supposed to. This simple shift in thought gives me an instant sense of calm, openness, and gratitude for whatever is going on in my life at that moment. When we are in a state of gratitude, The Universe brings us even more reasons to be grateful.

When you let go and let a guide in, it hits you: Your date last night was a disaster because it was going against the flow—nothing more, nothing less. The Universe was communicating, "Nope. Not now. Not you two." And so, it's not *you*, and it's not *the guy*. You are both beautiful individuals with much to offer *someone else*. On to the next.

When you let go of an unhealthy laser focus on the man you think you *must* have and instead tell The Universe that you trust it to MAN*ifest the man who is *right* for you, it will. (Remember, The Universe knows what we *need* more than we know what we *want*.) Setting your mind too intently on what you *want* closes you off to anything outside the box. The key is to open your heart to the infinite possibilities that are available for you and trust that The Universe will give you what you *need* for the relationship you ultimately desire.

FREE FALL INTO TRUST

Listen to how you talk about The Universe. Don't doubt it and don't nag it. The Universe is the ultimate master of logistics—it delivers all we need and want precisely on time. It is never too late and never too early.

How you surrender is up to you. How you tell The Universe you get it, you are all in, you are ready to rock, is your call. Go to the beach or the forest and scream into the wind. Write in your journal on one page or twenty who you are, who you are not, and who you would like to be with. Sing all the inspiring love songs or burn anything that you have in your possession that reminds you of your exes. Fill a bubble bath and close your eyes, have a dance party, or take a Zumba or art class. Do whatever you need to do to feel free.

OWN YOUR WORTH

To truly trust The Universe, remember the healing work you did in chapter 1. You've got to know deep down that you are worthy of a strong connection—of real, deep, mind-blowing love—and thus, The Universe will deliver it to you at the perfect time.

When you start to know your worth, it's a total game changer. When you start to let go of the reigns on a relationship and the need to control and KNOW everything, all the time, that's the place where a relationship has a chance to be in the flow—to unfold naturally and not through manipulation. Yes, manipulation. It's something we women have been taught to do from a young age to get guys to like us, to get them to do what we want, and to give us what we need. It's a tool The Control Freak loves to use, but it is depleting, just as Stephanie was learning. Manipulation is born from a desire for control, a desire to get what you want, yet it never feels good to get what you want through manipulation. It never creates anything authentic for anyone involved.

In my upcoming sessions with Stephanie, it became clear that she and I needed to work through two questions: Why was she so fixated on being with Jason? Why was she so comfortable with Jason treating her so poorly?

I had observed that Stephanie preferred talking about Jason over talking about herself, yet I knew that eventually through our work she would come to realize that people can't change other people. She can't change Jason, but she can change herself. However, we can only change ourselves if we shift our lens of perception and work to eliminate any negative narratives or limiting beliefs floating around in our brain.

As I encouraged Stephanie to open up to me about her own dating history, she brought up her struggle with her weight, something she'd been dealing with her entire life. When she started dating, she would take any guy who wanted her, because it meant she was good enough. She felt validated by them wanting her. But wanting her was just part of the battle. They then needed to deserve her and treat her right—something she didn't get yet. When Stephanie shared that her dad had struggled with alcoholism, I saw Jason's behavior was familiar to her. She had put up with and excused her father's behavior for years, which led her to do the same with Jason. Stephanie's father made her feel like she was worthless, and after years and years of that treatment, Stephanie started to believe she was worthless. She showed up in the world exuding the message, "You can treat me like trash, because I don't deserve to be treated any better."

Stephanie had no idea that she was sending this message. She thought she was a confident girl and that confidence allowed her to pursue "hot" guys like Jason. She could go after whomever she wanted and she chose Jason, but pursuing Jason kept her stuck in the same space she'd been in her entire life—the space of not feeling good enough, not feeling valued, and begging for love. There was a huge part of Stephanie that truly believed she couldn't do any better than how she'd already been treated. She stayed in the relationship with Jason because it hurt too much to say it wasn't right and wasn't working. She was afraid she wouldn't find another guy to "love" her. Stephanie was in "lack mentality" versus "abundance mentality."

The more stories she shared with me, the more I realized that she, too, was buying into the misbelief of "this time." "This time, he'll actually initiate. This time, he'll treat me the way I deserve to be treated. This time, he'll tell me he loves me when he's sober. This time, he will fall in love with me!"

Do you think anything ever changed with Jason?

Nope.

Let me say it again. We cannot control other people, and we cannot change other people. People are who they are, and it's our choice to either

1. love them unconditionally and accept them as they are, or
2. walk away and find someone else to love and be loved by.

FORGIVENESS LEADS TO FREEDOM

Stephanie was trying so hard to change Jason's nature, and it was causing her a tremendous amount of anguish. She couldn't see the similarities between Jason and her father. In fact, any time we talked about her father, Stephanie got visibly agitated. She didn't like revisiting this time in her life, but I needed her to know that not only do good guys exist but also she deserved to have one of her very own! It was her right as a human being on this earth to be in a loving relationship.

"Stephanie," I finally said, my smile oozing with compassion, "would you like to acknowledge the pain you felt in the relationship with your father so that you can heal and release it to arrive at the point of knowing that love doesn't have to look and feel this way?"

She looked out the window, tears brimming in her eyes.

"We can't control how we were treated in the past," I said. "We don't get a say over our parents, siblings, or our childhood. But we do get to realize when the stories we learned in the past are limiting our present and future. Would you like to invest in yourself and really start to work through all those feelings so you can start to create something different?"

She met my eyes with a small nod.

That morning, Stephanie began the work of forgiveness. She started with forgiveness toward herself for putting up with all the abuse in her past, and over time she was able to forgive her father. She realized that holding on to the resentment of how he treated her was only keeping her stuck in the past and made her replay it into the future and her relationships now. She began to embrace her true worth and claimed what she truly deserved, which was love: pure love, real love, love that feels good, is dependable, loyal, and something she can relax into. Not a love she needed to control.

While Stephanie worked on healing from her past and forgiving herself, Jason took a backseat in our sessions. After all, we were there to transform Stephanie, not Jason. About six months into our work together, just around the time where Stephanie had been showing some real self-love, she flew into our session with an announcement.

"Brace yourself!" she said, landing on the couch. "You're not going to believe what happened!"

It had been yet another week where Jason was avoiding her, so she'd come up with a new tactic she was eager to share with me.

"I got a burner phone with a new number, and I texted Jason pretending I was someone he'd connected with on Bumble…but they'd never met in person."

Her eyes were shining with what looked like triumph.

She then handed me the phone so I could read the exchange, where she pretended to be a woman named Jane.

Jane: So, are you seeing anyone?

Jason: I am seeing someone on and off, a cute British girl [Stephanie was relieved that he mentioned her]. I'm also dating a few other chicks [moment of happiness crushed].

Jane: Is this British girl special?

Jason: She's pretty special, but you know…

Jane: Are you in love with her?

Jason: No. Not her. I was in love with my ex, and I still think about her…

Jane: Do you think you could fall in love with the British girl?

Jason: I don't know—eh, probably not but I guess you never know. Probably not.

The conversation went on and on until this:

Jane: So, can I come over? I want to show you what I got!
Jason: Tonight?
Jane: Yes, tonight silly—I'm ready if you are!
Jason: I'm ready to go too!

At this point, it became clear that Stephanie, as Jane, wasn't about to go over there because, of course, she wasn't *real*.

Jane: Actually, I was just kidding—I'm tired—let's DO IT another night.
Jason: Oh, you got me all excited—OK, I guess another time.
Jason: You there?… Are you SURE you don't want to come over…??

I handed the phone back. Stephanie was slumped over on the couch, her whole body shaking, tears running down her cheeks. I could only imagine what it must have felt like for Stephanie to realize that Jason was obviously seeing other people and that he wasn't in love with her.

"I can't believe I'm even still crying. I feel like I shouldn't have any tears left after all he has done to me! How could he invite some random girl over when he tells me that he loves me and wants to marry me…when he is wasted…and only when he is wasted…but still?"

It was painful to see her in this place, but something had shifted. For the first time, instead of wanting him more because of his unattractive behavior and his unwillingness to fully commit to her, she found Jason's behavior unappealing. This final blow wasn't something she wanted to change. If this was how he was acting, she couldn't excuse it anymore. We were making progress.

After Stephanie's tears slowed, she smiled and said, "Well, I would like to give Jason *some* credit for telling Jane that he was seeing someone, 'a cute British girl.'"

Jason had told her he had always wanted to date a British girl, and Stephanie was his first.

"Wait!" she hollered. "Unless he started dating another Brit after he started dating me."

And...there it was again, the negative mindset trying to talk Stephanie out of her progress.

"No, who cares! If he wasn't talking about me, that would make it even worse. I'm DONE with him!"

And this time, she meant it.

And when Stephanie let go of the belief that Jason was The One, she was able to let go of Jason. Finally, she and I could begin the work of opening Stephanie up to the love The Universe had in store for her.

Stephanie ended things with Jason for good shortly after that session, because she wanted to meet the man she was supposed to be with! She continued coming to her weekly sessions with me and even went through a dry spell in her dating life—a first for her!—and she no longer tried to force things or control the outcomes. Her focus was on her continued healing, doing the deep work, and enjoying her life.

One day after work, she went to happy hour with a few of her friends. Minding her own business, on the way to the bathroom, she got stopped by a guy.

"Did you know that it's my friend Matt's birthday?"

Stephanie looked over to see his friend Matt and was instantaneously attracted to him.

"No, I didn't know that," she said to Matt's friend. "But happy birthday, Matt!"

Turns out, Matt had thought Stephanie was cute and had been planning to talk to her when his buddy decided to do it for him by making up that it was his birthday as a conversation starter. Stephanie was just as enamored and intrigued by Matt as he was with her, and they had an incredible night getting to know each other and having a lot of fun. Matt and Stephanie started dating. Matt was attentive, thoughtful, loving, and reliable, all foreign qualities to Stephanie, but she felt it in her heart that this was right. She felt at home with Matt, and she trusted him. She also kept herself open to the outcome of their relationship. She didn't want to get laser-focused again. She was going to relax, surrender, and accept all that might happen. If it didn't work out, she would be OK.

About ten months into dating, while on vacation in Mexico, Matt proposed to Stephanie.

These are always my favorite phone calls. It's when all the hard work—the pain and tears and heartache—ends in happily ever after.

Once The Universe senses that we are more at home in our own skin and at peace with our place in the world, it's invited to deliver our desires and to work its magic. When we are not so laser-focused and fixated, we give The Universe more space and more options to deliver what is meant to be. When we close the door on the past, that's when love comes into our lives. When we let go of our controlling instincts and trust, with eyes and hearts wide open, the gifts start flowing in.

Whatever story you are telling yourself about the current relationship you are in, whether you are home alone on a Friday night, unsure of when you'll meet someone who is worth going on a date with, or if you've just gone through a heart-wrenching breakup and you aren't sure if your heart can take any more, if you can let go of controlling the outcomes and move into the state of flow, trust, and excitement that your man is coming, then the struggle of dating dissipates. Instead, it becomes a journey of joy, hope, and enthusiasm.

He's on his way, loves. Sit with that. Trust that. There is nothing you need to do other than be open. Know that you are worthy. Get ready to watch it all unfold right in front of your eyes. Enjoy the ride—it's the most enjoyable ride of life.

CHAPTER FOUR EXERCISE: BE OPEN-MINDED

Are you ready to get past your laser focus and start the rest of your life? Fantastic!

*#1: Find a quiet place. Pull out your MAN*ifesting journal and a pen. Close your eyes and take a few deep breaths—just rest. Let your exhale last a little longer than your inhale as this leads to balance and relaxation. Allow any thoughts to come into your mind. Simply acknowledge them. Don't try to fight what comes up—just accept that it's there and allow your thoughts to pass through your consciousness.*

#2: When you feel at ease, call upon the name or the image of a man whom you feel you have been putting too much of your focus on as being the only option for your future. Do you see him? Good.

#3: Now, I want you to realize right now, in this moment, that there is more than one option for you and that no matter what happens with this man, your life will be marvelous. Take some time to make peace with the idea that you don't know and can't control what the outcome of a relationship with this man may be. Consider both possibilities in equal measure: (1) this man will become your future, or (2) he will not be a part of your future. Strive to be neutral and accept either outcome, because you know that The Universe will bring you what is for the highest good of all concerned, and it will bring you what you need.

#4: *Then, tell The Universe that you accept that it loves you, and you know it supports you. You accept that it will bring to you the best, most beautiful gem of a man—when the time is right. If the man The Universe brings you is not your "Plan A," (because he is The Universe's Plan B or Z), he will nevertheless be the perfect man—at the perfect time—for you. Sit with these thoughts until you begin to understand, believe, feel, and accept them. Relinquish any control that you perceived you had and feel the freedom of surrendering.*

#5: *Write down any feelings, thoughts, or insights that came up during the exercise. You might feel emotional. You might even cry tears of joy, because that often happens when you move from a place of fear and control into one of trust and surrender. Continue to connect to your breath, knowing that no matter how it works out, it will work out perfectly for you. You can do this exercise anytime you feel you have a tight grip on your relationship or a certain outcome.*

In the future, after your man has arrived safely and has been delivered into your arms, you can look back at this exercise in your journal and reflect on the moment you became open to infinite possibilities and the abundance of joy that is waiting for you. **This was the moment you fully surrendered to love.**

CHAPTER FIVE

Insight and Intuition

Affirmation: "*I completely trust my heart and my beautiful inner knowing.*"

IF YOU ARE GOING to MAN*ifest, you need to realize that YOU are the authority on how you feel and what you need to feel happy, fulfilled, and in love. Don't be The Settler: someone who tries to convince themselves that they've met the right person even though they know it is wrong deep down.

Years ago, back when I was dating a lot, I had a dream. I was sitting in my front yard with my back against the trunk of a tree. My entire front yard was jam-packed with people, looking like a mosh pit at Coachella, but instead of crowd surfing, I stayed seated, observing. My whole family was there, including all my ancestors. I saw all my friends and everyone I've ever known plus tons of people I'd never met. Everyone was yapping away, talking about me and telling me what they thought I should do and why.

When the voices, the sound, and the chaos became too much to handle, I stood up and started walking through the crowd, looking no one in the eye. I had a calling to exit what felt toxic and, at the very least, not helpful. I walked through the crowd with ease, staying in my peace, centered, and guided by my heart, knowing that all of these voices were destructive to my journey. Finally, past the crowd, I was met with an overwhelming sense of calm. The sun warmed my body, and I looked up at the most beautiful blue sky and glanced across the street. In the yard directly across from mine was a man. He was a gorgeous man, and I could sense his beautiful soul. At that moment, I knew that he was for me. I ran across the street into his arms, and nothing had ever felt better. We had come home to each other. We looked into each other's eyes, shared a magical kiss, and then my alarm went off.

I snoozed my alarm and tried so damn hard to go back to sleep, but the dream had woken me up. I had been relying on everyone else's opinions to help me through life instead of residing in my unwavering trust in myself. It was as though my intuition had been asleep up until that day, but then I woke up and never wanted to be "asleep" again!

Part of the process of MAN*ifesting is kicking the crowd off the driveway. Time to stop listening to others and start listening to yourself. Clear everyone and everything out of the way of your finding your man so you can think clearly, avoid red flags, and hone into what makes you happy. Time to start living your life for you and connecting your intention to your intuition.

Too many women push aside their intuition and spend months, sometimes years, with someone who doesn't treat them right, doesn't love them well, and isn't aligned with them energetically. They hang on to a mismatched man, convincing themselves that they've met The One even though they know deep down that that's not the case despite what other people might say.

If up until now, you've been listening to the voices of your family or friends, the ones telling you what they think of Peter or Max, then bless their souls but stop. These people are not *you*. You are the expert on you. You are the only voice you need to listen to when it comes to MAN*ifesting. Of course, you love your family and friends, but you know what's best for you. There's nothing wrong with telling your loved ones about a guy you're dating, especially if you're excited about him, but it's essential to set the boundary that you're not open to unsolicited relationship advice. If you ask for someone's opinion, that's different, but the only way that you're going to go from dating to destiny is if you trust yourself.

Trust yourself and you will attract the guy who is unequivocally aligned with you, in body, mind, heart, and soul.

Don't get me wrong—it's lovely to have a mature and healthy discussion with a loved one if you want to bounce something off them. The problem occurs when they give you relationship advice based on what they would do—based off their life experiences and who they are, which is a completely different person than you are with a completely different life. Your friends and family have the best intentions at heart, but hearing too many opinions will only cloud your own.

This is the reason I do not give advice to my clients. I let them come to their own discoveries and gain clarity without my influence so they can feel authentic empowerment. After hearing stories from distraught clients who have been suffering over what to do—keep dating the guy or move on?—I reflect on them with the utmost empathy (because I have been there and I know how terrible it feels). I tell them that I hear them, that I've listened to every word and felt every feeling they are feeling, and then I tell them that they don't have to suffer with this anymore. I offer my clients another way, which is not my way. We do a simple exercise, one that you can do too. Get comfortable, close your eyes, take a deep breath, settle into the moment, and get quiet. Breathe in through your nose and out through your mouth for a minute or two, which will regulate your nervous system and bring you to state of balance and serenity. Next, imagine that every factor, every person, every worry, every excuse—absolutely anything that is causing you suffering and indecision, anything that is in your way—has disappeared. Now...think of the man you are dating and tell me what you see, feel, and think about him.

Let me tell you, it's day and night. After this time to breathe and cleanse, everyone is more straightforward and articulate, and everyone speaks with authority. In fact, many women get very emotional because being that connected with yourself in your integrity is one of the best feelings on this planet.

RED FLAGS

Part of MAN*ifesting is feeling so strong and empowered inside, so aligned with yourself, your inner knowing, and your heart, that that's all that matters. Trusting yourself when you sense a red flag is what it's all about.

I met "Prince 38" in my early dating days. "Prince 38" was his Match.com name, and his profile stated that he was thirty-two years old. I wore something conservative yet sexy for our first date, and my self-talk reminded me that I was open and ready to explore this new person I was about to meet. I found out through our conversation that he went to some of the same schools my thirty-two-year-old friends did, so I thought it would be fun to play the "Do you know so-and-so" game to establish some sort of connection between us. He didn't know anyone. He went to the same small high school as my friend Howard and even the same overnight camp as my friend Alex, but he didn't know either one of them. And they were even the same age!

"You graduated high school in 1996, but you DON'T know either of these guys?" I asked, now just confused.

He shook his head. Apparently, the Prince did not.

As we continued chatting, something was off. Not just the people he'd never heard of, Prince 38 didn't connect with the zeitgeist of the era either. Something said he was inauthentic, that's for sure. My intuition was testing me, waving a red flag at me. Finally, I inquired as to how old he was.

Sheepishly, he said, "Thirty-eight."

Why did his profile say he was thirty-two when he is SIX years older than that? Then, in the most kind and sweet way possible, so as not to embarrass him, I asked why he was dishonest about his age, and "What was with the name 'Prince 38?'"

He explained that he wasn't dishonest because, even though his profile had his age marked as thirty-two, a potential date should have known he was thirty-eight years old. After all, his profile's name had the number "38" in it.

I nodded.

I see right through you, Mr. Stallion.

The rest of the date was awkward, with me trying to finish my glass of chardonnay as fast as possible. As chatty as I am,

I physically can't carry on a normal conversation once I know someone is lying. I took my last swallow, smiled, and then politely excused myself, explaining that I had an early meeting the following day. I couldn't wait to be out of his presence.

Admitting one's actual age on a dating site can be challenging. Above charm and good looks, above education and manners, I personally value honesty. It's a nonnegotiable on my list.

I had been dating Robert for several weeks. Initially, his fun, playful side allowed me to enjoy what was building between us, yet a part of me remained cautious. I saw a little red flag waving as I noticed inconsistencies. Very minor contradictions, but a red flag is a red flag.

One night after having sex, he said, "I have something to tell you."

Oh, no, I thought. Here we go. Is he dying? No, he seems fine. Does he have some kind of sexually transmitted disease? Oh G-d, please don't be that. Is he an "adult movie star?" Oy vey, please no! That would be a first.

"My birthday is coming up," he said. "And you are bound to find out my real age. I'm thirty-six."

This whole time he had me thinking he was two years younger than me when, in fact, he was three years older! I thanked him for being honest, cursed myself for not listening to my inner voice, and encouraged him to be honest about his age with other girls. I had no problem dating an older man. Unfortunately for him, he'd never know that.

There is no sense in being anyone or anything else than who you are. This is something that I was learning too.

Dear Intuition,

Please forgive me for being so slow to trust you.
Please forgive me for ignoring the red flags.

Love,

Jaime

Today my intuition is my best friend, and your intuition can be your best friend too. Get to know it. Listen to that voice inside, and you will never go wrong. It's there for a reason, and it will fly all those red flags, like dishonesty.

There is an acronym that I share with my clients when they question their red flags: **AVOID**.

A: Arrogant, otherwise known as "cocky." If you find that your date only talks about himself and brags a lot, then he's not your man. Arrogance is not attractive.

V: Violent. Do not let a man physically harm you—ever. Moreover, if you initially sense any violent tendencies, like a short fuse or easily angered, it will only get worse. You deserve more. Walk away.

O: Out of control. This could relate to his drinking or drug use, or it could relate to staying out late and not checking in. It means he is a loose cannon. "Thank you, next, please!"

I: Ignores you. This one can be hard to identify, but the overarching message is that if you don't feel like you are a priority, if the guy comes in and out of your life, ghosts you, disappears, and then comes back, he is up to something, and it's something that you don't need to take part in. You need a reliable, solid man who is consistent with his presence.

D: Dishonest. You can't trust this man. Whether it was a little lie (his age!), something bigger, or you feel something in your bones that says you can't trust him, know that it has nothing to do with an ex cheating on you or a parent being untrustworthy. This is a man you feel you can't trust. Listen to that gut feeling. Leave.

If you encounter *any* of these qualities in a man, run!

Maybe you've ignored or justified some red flags in the past. No sweat. We are all allowed to make mistakes. Forgive yourself and know you can begin to nip any potential or repeat mistakes in the bud. You can begin to pay attention to the good guys and the green flags. You are not here to settle for someone who doesn't celebrate all of you.

INTUITION

Red flags may get a bad rap, but they are markers for your intuition. You can allow the presence of these flags to honor and validate your feelings. Don't disregard them because that is disregarding your intuition, and that gut feeling is there for a reason. Have you ever stopped to think about why people say, "Listen to your gut," or "Trust your gut"? It's because your gut is your second brain. Neurotransmitters and hormones are produced in your gut and sent up to your brain; so, in many ways it is an alternative brain that operates on feeling versus thought.

Reflect upon your life for a minute.

Go back through your memories and see if there is a situation or experience in which you felt your gut tightening. How did that scenario play out? Was your gut brain trying to send a message that you shouldn't be doing something, that it's not right for you?

My spiritual psychology teachers Drs. Ron and Mary Hulnick introduced me to the term "sacred yes." A "sacred yes" is a "yes" that you feel throughout your mind, body, and soul. It's when you carry the knowing that it's something or someone that's right for you. Unless or until you feel that "YES," whatever or whoever it is should be a "NO." However, I must stress *unless* because in 99 percent of the situations, opportunities, and people you encounter you will know within the first few minutes whether it's a "yes" or a "no." It's a matter of learning to trust your intuition. It's also learning how to practice steadfast integrity. That means that you do what you know is right for you, *no matter what.*

"When you know, you know."

People say that all the time, but it's a real thing. Knowing is the sacred yes. Don't be The Settler, listening to others and convincing yourself you've found The One. Instead, continue on your MAN*ifesting journey guided by your intuition.

Many years ago, I was fixed up with a guy, Jeff, who came highly recommended. He was a very successful Hollywood agent who enjoyed taking me to special events, and it didn't hurt that Jeff was tall, dark, and so very handsome. He treated me like a princess. He wined and dined me at the most expensive and exotic places. It was my first "adult" relationship. I was intrigued and enjoyed all the attention.

After a few months, I began noticing unattractive behaviors. Jeff came across as intense, and his use of power was disturbing. He ordered a caprese salad, and when the waitress brought it in the traditional form—sliced tomatoes, basil, fresh mozzarella, and olive oil—he rudely sent it back because he had asked for diced tomatoes. I sat there thinking, *Is he serious? Can't he just cut the tomatoes up himself?* Maybe I was being punked. Another time, he realized he had missed his friend's birthday, and instead of calling his friend to apologize and wish him belated birthday wishes, he called his secretary to criticize her and yell at her for not reminding him. My red flags began to wave.

Just as I began to feel less romantic about Jeff, my parents began to picture us as newlyweds. When I explained how he could be dismissive, depressive, beyond high-strung, and just not enjoyable to be around at times (especially when he was drinking), my enamored parental unit would say things like, "Not everyone is perfect," and "It's hard to find a good guy." They saw what he was on paper, but they weren't the ones in the relationship, and yet I would still second-guess myself. *What's wrong with me that I don't see what they see?* That story is all too common.

I stuck it out for a while more. Sure, he offered a "fun" and extravagant lifestyle, but at what cost? Jeff kissed me like a vacuum cleaner. He sucked so hard that my lips would over-plump. I'm sure you're thinking, *Wait, don't we all want plump, voluptuous lips?* Yes, but not black and blue ones. I tell you, this man was intense. I would occasionally have to say, "OK, now you're biting." We had gone to New York for the industry upfronts: that's where the television networks introduce their new schedule to advertisers. This event had every opportunity to be fun.

There were loads of stars to get excited over, but that was not for me. And watching Jeff kiss ass to them was a bit sickening.

One night after a full day of television people, we went to a special restaurant he wanted to show me. He had invited a group of people, including one of his clients, a well-known television actress. Now, I was aware that he was working. However, our reservation was for eight o'clock at night, and we ended up waiting for his client, who showed up an hour and a half late, and the restaurant would not seat us until everyone had arrived. I was starving, and Jeff couldn't seem to care less. I did not feel taken care of whatsoever.

Jeff had just enough cocktails to give an exaggerated version of sucking up to his client as the dinner went on. Later, he was distant toward me. His "I'm too cool" persona came out whenever he drank. He was no fun. Red flags were hitting me on the head. I questioned myself as to why I was still in that relationship.

My guru-grandma heard me loud and clear. She suggested I break it off, but I didn't have enough courage at that point. I stayed with Jeff. He and I took a trip to Hawaii. My phone wasn't working, so I borrowed his for a few calls, but he got angry about how much data I was eating up.

"I think it's time to let go of Jeff," my brother said. "If you don't have a wonderful time with him in HAWAII, there's no reason to stay with him."

I agreed—and then I finally did it. Years later, I saw Jeff at a friend's birthday party. After some alcohol, he came up to me.

"You thought I was intense back then? I'm worse now."

By looking inside myself to understand why I didn't leave Jeff earlier, I know that others played a part in influencing me that he could be Mr. Right. My mom saw all the positive aspects he had to offer (on paper), and in her eyes, he had it all—great looks, an intriguing (albeit intense) job, and plenty of money to provide an affluent lifestyle. She couldn't see that we were missing a soul connection. But I knew pretty early on that he didn't display the qualities I enjoy in any man I'd be with. He didn't meet my nonnegotiables. He was the opposite of chill, modest, content, kind, thoughtful—and so-o-o far from fun.

It wasn't true love. I wasn't at home with him, and I knew it. It just took me a while to listen to my gut, take action, and move on.

VIBE AUTHENTICALLY

All living things are made up of vibrations. We are made up of vibrations. True love matches share similar vibrations. In honoring the law of attraction, the love you desire *will not* manifest if you exist on a low vibration and exude negative energy because that love won't match your inner world. If we set our intention to draw in a loving relationship, and we are getting red flags, heed their warnings—it's not a good vibration.

Don't be The Settler. That's not your vibration. Be authentic and work to see how you feel about yourself, how you've been treated, how you feel about your relationship, and how you are communicating what you desire to The Universe. If you want to MAN*ifest The One, then it's important to focus on what's inside you first. You need to check in with yourself, your patterns, your feelings, and your gut feelings frequently.

OLIVIA, THE SETTLER

Olivia grew up with an unreliable mom and a dad in the military. One could say that she had double unreliability with two absent parents. Her dad was never around, but her mother was and she treated Olivia, the oldest of three, differently than her siblings. Her mother relied on Olivia to be the "mom" in many situations, leaving Olivia to feel as though she couldn't rely on her own mom because her mom was always depending on her. Even though Olivia was only eighteen months older than her little sister Ivy, Olivia was expected to make dinner when her mom wasn't home from work, and she was forced to get a job in high school when her siblings never had to work. Olivia was always proving herself in an effort to win her mother's affection and attention. Straight *A*'s, valedictorian, head of the dance team, you name it, Olivia aced everything, but for every event that she had, her mom was obligated to be with her younger siblings. When Olivia was sad about a boy or got in a fight with a friend, she tried to go to her mom for support, to be held, to receive guidance, but her mother was always "too busy." Olivia's mom wasn't present physically, and she wasn't reliable emotionally—a double whammy.

Fast-forward to Olivia's early thirties. She was in the fashion industry, living in Paris, enamored by the French culture, and living her best life when she met Pierre. Olivia and Pierre had a magical and fate-filled beginning. It was Bastille Day, a day that Olivia had looked forward to her whole life, one much like the Fourth of July with many celebrations and fireworks—but in Paris. Her coworker Antoinette picked her up, and on the way to the festivities, they got a flat tire. Antoinette called her cousin Lou for help, but he was headed to the airport, so he sent his friend.

When Pierre showed up with a spare tire, a handsome face, and a killer smile, Olivia forgot about Bastille Day. She couldn't take her eyes off Pierre, who appeared equally smitten with Olivia. The girls invited him to join them for Bastille Day. Olivia and Pierre floated around from party to party into the early morning, ending up at a sunrise ceremony on the River Seine. Olivia did not want to miss it, and Pierre didn't hesitate to go with her. That morning the two wrote down their heartfelt dreams on pieces of paper and sent them off on little paper boats with hundreds of other people. They felt the magic of the moment and, more importantly, the magic of their meeting.

Olivia and Pierre had a storybook, year-long honeymoon phase in Paris, fell in love, and then moved to the US, to Olivia's hometown of Dallas. Now, Dallas is not the capital of fashion, but while in Paris Olivia started an international online clothing company, so she was a happy camper. Pierre, not so much. An experienced lawyer in Paris, he was having trouble getting a work visa, and at some point between the honeymoon phase ending, the culture shock of living in a different country, and the feeling of being out of work settling in, he, unlike Olivia, was not a happy camper, and his behavior changed.

When I asked Olivia if she had noticed any red flags earlier in the relationship, she said that looking back they were there, but she had rose-colored glasses on, so she didn't see them. She was never Pierre's priority. He was beyond flaky, basically unreliable, and she didn't feel like he had her back. She was putting more effort into the relationship than he was, yet nothing she did was good enough for him. He always had a negative comment about everything—from the meals she made to her success at work. Any outsider could see that this relationship was not healthy; however, Olivia was comfortable with this treatment.

Olivia manifested this relationship with Pierre because she never felt worthy enough of a solid presence and a loving connection. Acknowledging this fact and owning it was the only way that Olivia would heal, but I knew she wasn't there yet. She would make excuses for Pierre's behavior and had plenty of justifications for the relationship as a whole, constantly rationalizing why they should stay together.

"Pierre is having a hard time being away from Paris." (This doesn't excuse his behavior.)

"Pierre loves me. He is just sad, so it's OK for now." (It's never OK to be treated the way he was treating her. He had been unreliable and flaky and wasn't making her feel like a priority in his life.)

"But it was fate that we met, so there must be a reason we should stay together." (This was the most difficult one to argue.)

So, to that last one, I replied, "Yes, you had a magical meeting, but sometimes relationships are meant to happen for you to learn a life lesson. All relationships are meant to teach life lessons. The difference between this relationship and one that has endless potential is that this relationship lacks respect, honesty, a mutual valuing of one another, and unconditional love."

And from what Oliva reported, Pierre didn't believe in bettering himself. *He* didn't see a problem in the relationship, which is a sign that someone fears looking within to evolve in life and be the best version of themselves—very unattractive.

Just as Olivia had started to open her eyes and see that she deserved more than Pierre could ever offer her, she got pregnant.

"Maybe this is a sign that we are supposed to stay together," she said to me in one of our sessions.

About halfway through the pregnancy, Pierre said he couldn't stand living in the United States anymore, so he took off to Paris. Red flag alert: when two people are aligned in body, mind, and soul, they feel like home. This relationship was not home for either one of them. This was Olivia's wake-up call—the pain of feeling that not only was she not good enough for Pierre, but now his unborn child wasn't worth it to stick around.

Up until this point, Olivia's soul was doing anything possible to avoid doing the work to heal and in turn was resorting to living a life with a man whom, deep down inside, she knew she was settling for but couldn't stop herself. The insecure attachment to her parents is all she knew of love, and Olivia's relationship with Pierre mirrored her relationship with her mom. All roads led back to a feeling that no one had her back, that she couldn't rely on anyone, and no one truly loved her unconditionally. Not her mother. Not Pierre.

"Jaime, I've been settling for a relationship I wouldn't wish upon my worst enemy." Olivia was awake! "I deserve more. I've been selling myself short, and it has taken a long time for me to get here, but I finally get it. I completely understand why I manifested Pierre, why I stayed so long, and now, what I'm supposed to learn—that I will never again settle for anything less than what I deserve."

I was smiling.

"I need to start treating myself better for a man to treat me better and, most importantly, to trust my intuition if something doesn't feel right."

It took Olivia some time to hit her rock bottom and have her aha moment, but she got there. Something inside of her—her intuition—said, "Enough is enough."

When her son Krieger, which means "warrior" in German (honoring her heritage), was a year old, Olivia decided it was time to start dating again. This girl was pumped up and ready.

Before Olivia could truly MAN*ifest, she needed to let go of a negative narrative that she had regarding men. Olivia wanted to be with a financially secure man, but she was worried that if a man had money, that meant that he wasn't going to prioritize her, and he would probably be really cocky and vain. I saw this story as a block for her.

"Olivia, can you tell me why you have made this assumption?"

"Well, I've never seen a couple where the man is successful and kind to his wife as well. Most couples I have seen where the man is successful, he is either working all the time and doesn't prioritize his wife and family or he is just disrespectful and criticizes his wife."

I explained to her that she *can* have both: a successful and kind man. I asked her if she was open to doing an experiment. She was intrigued and agreed to try one.

"If it's going to help me find my man, I'm down for anything!"

"Fantastic!" I cheered enthusiastically. "I know you said you did not know any couples who have what you're looking for; however, I'd like you to take a moment and really think about that for a second. Close your eyes and think of any couple you know, personally or from a distance, where the man at least appears to embody the qualities you're looking for and the couple appears to be happy, because of course you never know what goes on behind closed doors."

I asked Olivia to take a moment, center herself, take a few deep breaths, and then see what came forward for her. After about a minute, she grinned and opened her eyes.

"It looks like you might have found a couple in your memory vault."

"Actually, I don't know why I didn't think of them before, but my client Isabelle and her husband, Andre, are very happy, and I know this because I have spent time with them at dinners and parties in the past. I haven't seen them in a few years so they didn't pop into my consciousness until now. Andre runs his own real estate business and is very successful. He also happens to be an incredibly devoted husband and father."

"OK, so we are making progress," I replied. "I'm giving you homework. I want you to continue to brainstorm couples who can be a model for what you're looking for. I want you to make a visual representation of the relationship that you desire to manifest into your life. Collect pictures of these couples and put them all together in a collage. Place the collage on your wall or on your nightstand. You can also take a picture of it so you can have it on your phone. I want you to be able to see this collage on a daily basis to remind you that what you are looking for does in fact exist, and if it happened for all of those women, it could happen for you too!"

Olivia obliged.

The next session, Olivia walked in with a gorgeous collage. She is quite artistic and really went the extra mile. She took me through each couple and told me about why she chose them. She had about fifteen couples ranging from Isabelle and Andre to Ron and Mary Hulnick (my spiritual teachers, whom she knows), to Mila Kunis and Ashton Kutcher and Kyra Sedgwick and Kevin Bacon. Although she doesn't know some of the couples personally, she has read enough of about them to infer that they generally have happy and healthy marriages.

Olivia was a terrific "student" and looked at that collage every night before she went to sleep. She sent herself off to dreamland in a positive manner, visualizing her ideal dark-skinned, nature-loving, creative, *handsome*, and successful man. She was looking for a very particular man, aesthetically speaking. She took out her phone and showed me an Instagram page that was for men who were on a self-evolution journey; men who weren't afraid to be vulnerable; conscious men. Many of the men had a certain look that Olivia melted over. I encouraged her to pick a guy and "slide into his DMs," but she didn't feel quite there yet and I honored her self-recognition. She did, however, start to use a few dating apps, which she was excited about. Olivia was on a journey. At least she knew what she was looking for, and when the time was right, it would happen. Well, that time came quicker than both of us thought it would.

One day, she came into my office with the biggest grin on her face.

"Jaime, this is a different ballgame I'm playing now. I am so in tune with my intuition. Even from the time I see a guy's profile on an app, within thirty seconds I get a sense of whether he is a 'yes' or a 'no.' I've been on so many great dates. You were always right; you said that when my inner world shifted, so would my outer world."

Olivia went on to find her soulmate, Jeremy, on Bumble, and he looked exactly like he could have been one of those guys on Instagram. As much as she wanted to meet him organically and have a romantic "fate" story to tell their kids (they now have two, and he legally adopted Krieger), she was happy that they had found each other.

That's all that matters. Two people finding each other is the first step to the rest of their lives, and when you have a love like Olivia and Jeremy have (I got to witness it at their wedding), the details of how they came to be just fade away.

Before we move on from discovering the power of your intuition when it comes to MAN*ifesting The One, it's important that you discern the difference between your intuition and the sabotaging ego voice in your head that brings up all the old stories and judgmental self-talk.

I had a client who broke up with her boyfriend because she felt she wasn't good enough for him. Tim grew up with an abundance of privilege, and Delaney did not. She thought that he was more intelligent than her. After all, Tim had his master's degree. He was well-traveled and very successful. Because of all this outside (materialistic) stuff, she forgot about the importance of the inside stuff—her inside and his—and that's all that matters when it comes to compatibility and chances for long-term success. So, Delaney made up a story in her mind that Tim was too good for her, and she believed it. The truth was, he never once made her feel any less important than him. He did the opposite. He made her feel like a princess. He showed her nothing but respect and love, but she had a hard time believing that it was sincere and that she deserved it.

When Delaney would talk about the relationship, I could tell how much she fell in love with this man by how she spoke about their time together, and it took several sessions to figure out that she was giving herself the secret, self-sabotaging "not good enough" reminder. The fact that he was an intellectual impressed her; it made her happy. She loved that about him, but she felt inadequate around him, and it might be safer to let this one go, break it off before he could. She was sure that he would inevitably wake up one day and realize that he was too good for her. That way, she wouldn't have to feel embarrassed about her measly bachelor's degree and her job as a hairdresser or the fact that she was from a small town with one stoplight as opposed to the affluent city her beau was from. Delaney was letting her fear lead and her ego raise red flags.

Our inner thoughts are often faster than what we can keep up with, which is why we must make it a habit to look inside to see "the why" of the decisions we make as much as possible. The answer is always there. It may be hiding, so we must be diligent in checking in with "the boss."

When you find yourself dating a challenging person, look at what it is about him that you don't like. What is triggering about him? You will find that it is often a projection of something that is going on within you, an old, untrue belief from your past or self-sabotaging ego. Or it can be as straightforward as what we don't appreciate in others is something we don't like about ourselves.

I'm sure you know by now that not every date or meetup in Paris ends in love. Some people come into our lives for karmic reasons. They come into our lives to teach us something about ourselves. While going through the relationship may not be fun, we must have these experiences. I like to think that we signed up for everything before coming to this earth. We must peel back every layer of that onion to get to the core of our true self.

CHAPTER FIVE EXERCISE: BE SELF-TRUSTING

Since we now know that everyone is born with intuition, it's just a matter of strengthening your intuitive muscle to create a stronger connection.

In order for your intuition to be extra on point in your romantic life, it helps to practice listening to your intuition in all areas of your life. Try this exercise of getting in touch with your intuition over the next month and see how your intuition grows and your life and relationships improve.

#1: When you're at a restaurant and you can't decide what to get, stop asking your friends or the waitstaff. Ask yourself: What do I want to eat right now? Your answer will always be there, whether it's the organic grass-fed steak or the tofu stir-fry that you choose, because you're in tune with your intuition and you're in tune with what you know is the best decision for you.

#2: Focus more on your internal compass. When you have free time and you don't know what to do, don't ask someone else to make plans or what they want to do. Ask yourself: What do I want to do right now?

#3: Now, it's time to home in on your intuition for your dating journey. When you're swiping on your app, slow down. Close your eyes, look within, and feel the guy's energy. You'll know right or left.

#4: Before your date, get centered and grounded. You can do this by closing your eyes and breathing or by going outside and

touching the earth. Essentially you don't want to feel like your head is up in clouds; you want to be in your body. You should be fully present on the date, so you're able to have a clear path to your intuition and your heart.

On your date, in every moment, I want you to look inside and ask yourself, is this a "yes" or a "no"? When you're connected with your intuition, you'll know how you feel.

The more practice you have asking your intuition, the stronger your intuition will become. Look at this as a game. Have fun. When you encounter new men, practice using it.

Does he feel like a good person to you? Is he someone you feel comfortable with, or do you get a sketchy or creepy vibe? Do you feel lit up and alive when you see him? Trust your answers! Trust you. You are your authority, and your clarity is always there, waiting for you to get quiet enough to hear and feel it.

CHAPTER SIX

Believing, Knowing, and Visualizing

Affirmation: "*I feel full of love and happiness, living my life as if my person is already in it.*"

HEARTBREAK ISN'T EASY, BUT it's something that all of us will experience in our lives. I can't tell you how many times I was on such a high that came crashing down because a guy decided that I wasn't the right girl for him. My clients too. We aren't good enough, pretty enough, happy enough, and the list goes on. Then, I see my guy with *another girl*. What does she have that I don't have? I took it to mean something about me, but all it meant was that we weren't right for each other. As much as I told myself he was making a mistake—because how could he not feel what I was feeling?—and as much as I thought I knew what was best for me, I had to learn how to surrender and say, "OK, Universe, I trust that you know what you're doing. I believe my guy is out there."

The Universe wants us to be happy. It's constantly rooting for us and arranging things divinely so that we can be happy— we just need to trust that it is doing so.

The Universe is waiting to deliver your desires, and I am here to help you avoid any more pain and suffering when it comes to love, or at least shorten the duration of heartbreak after a breakup. I know that you wouldn't be reading this book if you didn't feel like you have already suffered; so, you've put your time in, girl. Enough is enough. The next time (if there is a next time, because who knows, maybe the next man that comes into your life is The One) a man lets you know that you're not right for him, the next time a man is giving you his spiel, pretend that he is Charlie Brown's teacher. It's all gibberish, and all you have to do is nod your head.

But then, just before you part ways, I want you to imagine he's handing you an envelope. You open it up, slide out the paper, and read the letter.

> *Dear Incredible, Beautiful Inside and Out, Intelligent, Fun, Funny, Interesting, and WORTHY Woman,*
>
> *It's me, The Universe. I'm just letting you know that you just dodged a bullet. He was not your person. I know it's hard for you to see now, but believe me when I say this. Trust that I will deliver your man to you, and he will be the right man at the right time. You will look back at this relationship as just a blip in the journey of your extraordinary life. This man that I'm going to bring to you, OMG—what you felt for your ex*

will not even come close, like I'm talking not within a billion miles, to how much you're going to feel for The One.

I cannot wait for that day for you. It's coming. I cannot wait to see you light up and feel alive! But here's the ticket. Listen carefully. You need to light up and feel alive before he comes into your life. Can you do that for me? No matter what is going on in your outside world, I want you to feel lit up and alive and LOVING yourself, NO MATTER WHAT, because that's when I'll know you're ready.

Sending love and light to you, the badass goddess that you are!

Love,
The Universe
PS: You're welcome!

BELIEVING

It might be hard to imagine, but you need to be able to see at least a glimmer of hope. You need to see it happening, because once you see that glimmer, the glimmer can turn into a possibility, and that possibility can turn into a belief, which becomes your reality. Then, *boom!* you find yourself having MAN*ifested.

Believing is the core element to MAN*ifesting. It is not just something to help you heal heartbreak. You must believe that you're going to meet your man to meet him. You need to believe that you deserve the great love that is in store for you in order to receive it. You need to remind yourself on the daily that there is a man out there who is looking for you—just like you are looking for him. Whatever it is about you that makes you who you are is what that man is looking for.

Now, you might find yourself straying from the path here and there, meaning that you will drop into your humanness and regress in your self-work at times. You might hear some negative narratives, even those that you had already resolved as The Faultfinder.

But you have the power. Anytime you backslide, step up and repeat: "I believe."

Possibility leads to belief, and belief leads to knowing, and you need to know that you're going to meet your man. Knowing that it will happen is crucial MAN*ifesting energy. It's as if you are having a premonition. It is potent. Nothing can stand in the way of your knowing and it happening. When you know something will happen, it can't *not* happen. Knowing is unadulterated, unwavering belief in The Universe that what is for you will never pass you by, never.

KNOWING

Travel back in time for a moment to visit that little girl who had big dreams. The one who would play dress-up and house and talk with friends about the guy she was going to marry, the house she was going to live in, and the kids she was going to have.

When you were little, there was no doubt in your mind that you would get married to a wonderful man, a man who you loved to see at the end of the day, a man to see the world with and have adventures, a man who would be there to support you and you to support him—a man who made you happy. That man is still there, and there is no number of bad relationships that can keep you two apart. Tap back into that knowing right now. He is still there. He hasn't gone anywhere. I don't care if you've already been married and have a child or two or five—or if he has! When two souls are supposed to be together, they will be.

Go back to that little girl who was brilliant at playing pretend: fairy princesses, cats and dogs, chefs, doctors, and dancers. She was so good at seeing herself as what she knew she could be. We are born visualizers. We can create scenes and scenarios in our mind that feel as true as our reality. We can do this to our detriment but also to our fulfillment.

VISUALIZING

You start to imagine and *see* what your life will be like with your man. Why is it so important to see yourself and pretend what it will be like to be with your man? Well, for one, it will feel incredible. And two, visualization is a core element to MAN*ifesting. Not only is The Universe always listening to you, but neuroscientists have also proven that visualization changes lives by changing neural pathways. The brain doesn't know the difference between what is happening in the present moment versus what happened in the past and what will happen in the future. All it knows is what you feed it.

For example, suppose you are living in the past and making yourself crazy over wishing that things could have been different. In that case, you will continue to give The Universe reasons to believe that you are still there with your ex, hoping for it to work out, which is why it can't possibly bring The One forward to you. However, if you can be in the present moment, you will be able to drop the past and visualize what life will be like with your man. The more you can start living as if he is already in your life, the faster he will appear because, as you already know, The Universe gives us what we focus on.

"What does visualizing my man look like, Jaime?"

I get this question a lot from my clients. I can only imagine you are asking it too.

From this day forward, I want you to live your everyday life pretending that your man is already here with you. OK, wait a minute. Let me clarify. I am not saying start introducing your imaginary boyfriend to people in line at the coffee shop. Please don't take it that far. What I want you to do is incorporate a nameless, handsome fellow into your life.

First, get daydreamy. What would it be like to wake up in the morning next to him? What would it be like to have dinner together, to visit your favorite local spots, to sleep next to him, for him to pet your cat—whatever you can dream up? Talk to his soul and tell him how grateful you are to have him in your life. Feel his arms around you, spooning and laughing when you wake up in the morning. Visualize your physical connection. Use your imagination. Imagine having as much sex as you want with him. Or imagine how you have never felt so connected with someone, how amazing it will feel for your bodies to be connected in that way, and how incredible it will feel to be held by him. Imagine going on vacations together, going to the grocery store, and picking him up at the airport when he gets home from a business trip. Imagine going to parties together and watching movies at home. Imagine building a life together—the kids, the house, the love, *all* of it.

Now, bring him into your reality. At night, undo his side of the bed. When you set up a place setting for yourself for dinner, set one for him too. You can even pour him some wine. Make sure that your living space says, "Open for business." Clear a little space for him in your closet so The Universe knows there's room for him. When you're out having fun with your friends, imagine checking your phone to see the sweet text he sent you saying he hopes you're having fun and can't wait to see you when you get home. Live as if in all aspects of your life he is there. You catch my drift. Live as if he is in your life today and see through your mind's eye and feel into your heart's desire what life will be like with him throughout your relationship.

Feel the joy for how lucky you are to have found him. Feel your heart at peace. Feel your nerves relax. The search is over. You can rest.

I attended a media conference in New York City called "Unfair Advantage Live," hosted by media moguls Jen Gottlieb and Chris Winfield. Besides learning a lot about marketing and PR (entirely out of my wheelhouse), I got the privilege of getting to know Jen and Chris and hearing their life stories. They are an engaged couple, and Jen absolutely MAN*ifested Chris. On day one of the conference, on the gigantic screen in the front of the room during Jen's story, she shared a list of qualities she was looking for in her future man. The list had thirteen items on it, and it was very specific. As she went through each item, I watched Chris to see his smiling face as Jen went through the list and lit up more and more after each one she listed because Chris is everything on her list and more. It was a moment for them, and it was a moment for all of us, witnessing their epic connection. Jen was very clear on who she was looking for. With utter conviction, she consistently imagined him in her life, visualizing as if he was already in it, and voila, he showed up, and both of their lives were changed for the better.

MADISON, THE MISS BELIEVER

My client, Madison, was thirty-four when she came into my office. Unbeknownst to Madison, she embodied the Miss Misbeliever dating persona. She was living at a low vibration and stuck in misbelieving land.

Through no fault of her own, The Miss Misbeliever is someone who either has never had a model of a soulmate-esque relationship or no longer believes in that possibility. This person grew up with parents who were either miserable and stayed married or divorced but continued to fight. She has never witnessed a healthy and thriving relationship, and for that reason has yet to have a healthy romantic relationship in her own life. Because, The Miss Misbeliever will claim, how can you have a healthy relationship if you don't believe they exist?

Or The Miss Misbeliever can be a woman who came from a loving relationship and believed in love but has since had a traumatic experience or a series of negative relationships that have jaded her belief in love. Now, when she sees a happy-looking couple on the street, hears her friend talk about her relationship, or watches a TV show or movie that portrays a happy couple, she thinks, *That doesn't exist. They must be hiding their hatred and resentment toward one another.* Or, *That's nice, but it won't last for long.*

When I encounter a client who is The Miss Misbeliever, it's my job to help them heal the unresolved issue associated with their romantic dissolution, getting them to a place where they can start to believe that there are happy relationships in this world and that they are not an exception. The Universe did not leave them out, and there is a happy relationship waiting for them as well.

As a child, Madison, now thirty-five, was the opposite of this dating persona—she was a Miss Believer! She was a romantic who watched every rom-com ever made, and although she was bullied in school and didn't date a lot until college, she remained positive and hopeful until one night changed her entire outlook on dating and men. Madison was date-raped. She was twenty-five, and it happened with a guy she trusted, someone whom she had known for years. He was a few years older and had gone to her high school. They went on a date, drank a lot, and went back to his apartment. They started fooling around, and Madison could sense that things were starting to progress, but she wasn't comfortable with that. She never slept with guys on the first date, and she wasn't going to start, so she told Nick that she didn't want to have sex with him. It fell on deaf ears. She pleaded with him only to realize that she was not going to win—he wasn't letting her move. Madison then dissociated and emotionally left her body until it was over. She did the best she could, feeling safer letting him proceed—still without consent—because she believe that he'd get violent if he didn't get his way.

Everyone's rape story is different; however, the one truth that runs throughout is that it should not happen—to anyone—ever! Yet it continues despite the #MeToo and women's rights movements. With all this awareness and conversation, you would think that men would know that it's not OK to violate a woman. The unfortunate truth is that these are men who have unresolved issues that they've never looked at and, as we know, "hurt people, hurt people." I'll never understand how someone can violate another human being like that. I pray that someday it will stop or there will be harsher consequences, so perhaps men will think twice before committing such a heinous act.

If you are a rape victim or have experienced any type of trauma, know that it was not your fault. You did nothing wrong, and healing is on the other side; you're on your way. As my incredible teachers Drs. Ron and Mary Hulnick say, "Healing is the application of loving to the places inside that hurt." Loving yourself is the gateway to the rest of your life.

After the incident, Madison built a wall around her heart and extrapolated how she saw that man onto all men. She no longer believed that good men were out there, and if they were, they wouldn't want her. For the next ten years, she rarely went on a second date because she was so closed off. Her sweet and inno-cent heart was broken. She was angry and resentful that the rape happened, and she didn't know how she could ever find love.

Eventually, she started therapy because even though she was operating as The Miss Misbeliever, a tiny part of her knew this couldn't be all there was to life. Madison had no clue how she was going to believe in love again, so we started slowly, taking tiny little steps. She recounted the story. She cried, grieved her innocence, and bargained, wishing that the past could change, but the pivotal moment for her was when she found acceptance. She accepted what had happened could never change, but that she did have the power to change her outlook. She did have the power to stop giving any more energy to that man and to stop letting her past dictate the rest of her life. Session by session, she opened her heart and let down her walls. She began healing.

Healing is not a walk in the park. It's hard. However, healing is the greatest investment in yourself you will ever make. One of the reasons I wrote this book is to help you realize that you are the most investable commodity in your life. The more you invest in yourself, the more you will see your ROI shoot through the roof. The ROI is the feedback from The Universe that you are on your way. Feedback is a wonderful man showing up on your Bumble app, an opportunity out of the blue to be on your dream podcast, or someone you're still in love with coming back into your life. When you elevate, the world elevates with you.

Madison did the hard, healing work.

"I want to be a coach and help people heal their trauma," Madison shared with me during one of our sessions. "I will not rest until everyone who has experienced trauma knows that they can heal, just like I did."

Madison is not the first client of mine who has been so inspired by her own healing that she decided to help other people as well.

Once Madison was on the other side of her trauma, she was ready to dive back into dating again—and she was a quick study. I called her my "little grasshopper." She immediately put her love life into action. Madison set her intention for meeting her soulmate and used all the MAN*ifesting tools to bring in her man.

She loved my idea of setting a place at dinner for her "person." She took it to another level, though. Madison lived in a high rise in New York City. She wanted to get as close to The Universe as possible, so it could really hear her, so she would have dinner with her imaginary boyfriend on her balcony every night she was home for dinner. She would set out their plates and imagine what it would be like to be sitting there with him, laughing, having intriguing conversations, and flirting. She imagined discussing her day with him and hearing about his. She imagined planning their future together, taking vacations, and all of it filled her heart with joy.

Remember that the brain doesn't know the difference between what is happening in real life and what is imagined, so after about six months of Madison's "spiritual experiment," she found herself on a date with a tall and handsome lawyer. Nathan was intelligent and athletic, and he had a great sense of humor—Madison adored him!

At first, Madison had a rough time trusting that he was a genuine man. She was waiting for something to go wrong. At any moment, he was going to reveal that he was just an avatar. "Nathan" would lift off his mask to reveal a monster or the Hulk or some sort of scary creature. I encouraged her to be honest with Nathan, to share with him that she was doing her best to keep her heart open and to trust and believe that he was the real deal. Every time Nathan would take care of her, he would reassure her that he wasn't going anywhere, that her past didn't scare him, and that he loved her for all that she is. Slowly, Madison began to believe that his goodness wouldn't disappear, and they went on to have a healthy relationship supported by couple's therapy to help them both set up a foundation. It took a few years, but Madison's dating persona shifted from Miss Misbeliever to Mrs. Believer, or more specifically, Mrs. Nathan Hall.

More often than not, it is not our present situation that makes us nonbelievers. Like Madison, it's the past that turns out to be the biggest block to becoming Mrs. Believer. We can be so wrapped up in the past that we're too busy or too afraid to look at our life now and see that healing is possible.

HEALING THE PAST

Leaving your past in the past is not easy. However, when you have unflappable trust in The Universe, past hurt can fade. In fact, when you believe that The Universe can deliver your desires, you don't have to do as much work on releasing the past as you may think.

I'm sure you've heard of "cutting the cord." Many a relationship therapist, coach, love guru, and so on will advise you to cut the imaginary cord you have with your ex—or any man you felt an enormous amount for in your past. I am *not* going to tell you to cut the cord. Nope, I'm going to ask that you do the opposite; when my clients hear this, they let out an immediate sigh of relief. I can always feel it too. A weight they held on to for so long is lifted off their shoulders. Many have been trying and trying to cut that cord—sometimes cords.

I had been crying buckets to my friend Simon about Ben. Simon was a trusted colleague and fellow coach, and I could not stop my tears. I kept going on and on about cutting the cord, trying to prove to him that I was doing everything possible to cut through my feelings for Ben. *How did I still have feeling for him?*

"Simon, I bet you no one has had this hard of a time getting over someone," I said, going into victim mode. "People go on with their lives, and they find their person. I know that I have to stop my feelings for Ben or else I'll never find my man."

Simon listened for a while and then, in the kindest way possible, looked me dead in the eye.

"Stop."

I was taken aback.

"What? Why?"

"What if you don't have to cut the cord?" Simon asked. "What if your feelings are still there to remind you what your heart can feel? What if they remain to keep your heart open to love?"

Simon was onto something.

Like my clients now, I felt free from the impossible burden I was bestowing upon myself. I felt liberated and validated like it was OK—more than OK to have feelings for Ben still. I'll never forget that moment, and I'll be forever grateful to Simon for helping me open my eyes and keep my heart open. Up until that moment, I had been distraught for years over the heartache of ending of my relationship with Ben. I had been trying every-thing to not care about him anymore. When I say *everything*, I'm talking psychics, coaches, therapists, anyone! I went to a sha-man, and she allegedly cut the cord, but that didn't work. I had a burning ceremony with my friends (just like Rachel, Monica, and Phoebe!), but that didn't work. I burned all the pictures I had of us and all my journals that had every detail of every moment I spent with him, because the psychic told me to do it. She believed my feelings would magically disappear by doing so, but that didn't work. I was told by so many people that if I didn't cut the cord then I was holding myself back from my future and The One. I *had* to get rid of the feelings.

But Simon told me something different—which is exactly what I share with my clients and now you. Of course, you don't want to dwell in "shoulda, woulda, coulda" land because that's not healthy either. What is healthy is having radical acceptance of everything that has happened and believing that it's for the highest good. When you cut the cord, you lose the benefits of feeling, and we want to keep feelings because you can use those feelings to MAN*ifest the right man.

These are the feelings that raise your "heart bar." You have experienced a certain feeling in the past, and now you know what it feels like to be in love. You know what it's like to feel strongly and deeply for a man. Thanks to my relationship with Ben, my heart experienced more than it ever had. I was intrigued, in love, and I could not get enough of him. I had learned what it's like to feel an outer-worldly connection with someone. If I had forced myself to shut *all that* down, my heart would've settled for any man, because I would have erased those feelings and lowered my bar back to the pre-Ben days.

Instead, my "heart bar" was raised, and I wasn't going to get married until I felt that or something more. It happened when I met my husband, Bryan. I held out and waited—I didn't want to settle because after feeling what I felt for Ben, I couldn't end up with just *any* man; he had to be special.

Yes, absolutely, take the necessary steps to heal your past. Reflect, grow, learn, evolve, get empowered, but that doesn't mean forcing yourself to forget your past. Move on from the pain but keep the pieces that felt like heaven. You're going to need them. If you've been struggling to "cut the cord" from your ex or your past in general, you can stop. If you force yourself to negate those experiences and cut off from those feelings, then your "heart bar" will plummet. Great love grows from the inside out, so you want to be able to keep those feelings alive so that when you meet a man who you feel is for you, you will be able to recognize it. Keeping the feelings is a reminder to yourself of what your heart is capable of feeling. My dear friend Julia, who is a widow, so beautifully explained what she felt for her late husband, and I think it's a perfect example of a deep-rooted and undeniable love. "Loving Daniel made me feel like I grew an extra chamber in my heart; that's how much I loved him." Julia's breathtaking description eloquently describes the feeling that you should look for as you are MAN*ifesting.

Love is the seed, the source of all that grows. Life is the juicy grapes, the winding vines, the broad leaves, and the penetrating roots. Cut yourself off from the source, and there will be no soil to grow from.

CHAPTER SIX EXERCISE: BE-LIEVE

As we know, the brain doesn't differentiate feelings between an imagined experience and a real experience. The more the brain gets used to firing those "feel good" neurons, the higher your vibration will be. We MAN*ifest love when our vibration is high, when we are in the flow of life, and we can use the power of visualization to raise our vibration.

In this exercise, I'll introduce you to Ideal Scenes.

Visualizing is a powerful step in MAN*ifesting, but (to review), you can't just visualize; you need to believe and know that it's going to happen.

I first leaned about Ideal Scenes during my spiritual psychology studies at the University of Santa Monica. An Ideal Scene can be about anything that you want to manifest, so for our purposes we are MAN*ifesting The One. Your Ideal scene will center on your future man. What will your life be like together? You want this to be very detailed. An ideal scene centers on what you do want, not what you don't want.

#1: Create a blank slate. This can be either a page in your notebook or a posterboard you hang on your wall. At the top, write down what you are going to call your Ideal Scene. For example: "Incredible Relationship with My Beloved Husband." Below your title, write the following words: "This or something better for the highest good of all concerned."

#2: Draw a heart in the middle of your page or posterboard. Write the words "I am" in the middle of the heart.

#3: *Imagine your heart as the center of the wheel or the center of the sun. Then, like spokes of a wheel or rays of the sun, write sentences coming off the heart. Each sentence describes what you desire in your ideal relationship and what qualities The One possesses. Think of each spoke or ray as a statement to The Universe that describes how the relationship exists in real time. Here are some examples:*

- *"I am enjoying an authentic romantic relationship with my man who sees me, hears me, and accepts me for all that I am."*

- *"I am grateful for the ability to travel with my husband, and we love seeing the world together."*

- *"I am loving the fact that I am crazily attracted to my husband, and we have a very plentiful and active sex life."*

- *"I am feeling lucky to be experiencing a life of abundance and financial freedom with my husband."*

- *"I am having FUN with my man, and we are always laughing together."*

#4: *Put your Ideal Scene on your nightstand or hang it on your wall—anywhere you can read it every night before going to sleep!*

#5: *Before bed, close your eyes and ask The Universe to bring your Ideal Scene into your life. Also, if there's anything that you need to know or do to make that happen that you don't know or are not doing already, ask The Universe to please show you* *in a way that you can understand. Remind The Universe that you are grateful, and you believe that it will bring to you what you need, not necessarily what you want. And then send that prayer into the light.*

CHAPTER SEVEN

The One Before "The One"

Affirmation: "*I am willing to share all parts of me with no attachment to the outcome. By sharing my authentic self, I can deeply connect with the man I am destined to be with.*"

VULNERABILITY IS THE KEY to connection, and it is essential on your MAN*ifesting quest. Learning to be vulnerable is one of the most life-changing gifts you can give yourself. Practice vulnerability and you will share your soul—and you will invite the person in front of you to share their soul.

Many of us don't know how to be open. In fact, we fear scaring people off with our feelings. But the truth is, you cannot hold back if you're going to manifest true love. I'm not saying go all in sharing every feeling you've ever felt on the first or second date, but a relationship requires that you learn to be honest with yourself and honest with the person you are dating. Vulnerability is where the depth of connection is born.

In this book, you've come far on your MAN*ifesting journey. You've learned to work through your issues to show up authentically. You've ditched the limiting stories. You've gotten back to the source of who you are. You've determined what you are looking for and what you want. You've let go of your laser focus so you can surrender and flow toward your person.

Now it is time to get over yourself, get out of your own way, and be open, be raw—be vulnerable.

You have nothing to lose, but you'll gain everything you've ever wanted.

Most of us were not brought up to be vulnerable, and it's no fault of our parents, as they were doing the best they could. I was taught, and I saw it modeled as I grew up, not to let people know any negative feelings. And it's not that anyone told me not to share my positive feelings either, but there wasn't anyone encouraging us girls to open up and share our feelings with guys because "he should tell you how he feels first." It's not society's fault either. Everything comes in divine timing, as you know, and we are finally living in a time when vulnerability is shining. It's a current buzzword and the limelight is fairly new, but being real and raw is compelling because a surface relationship just doesn't cut it.

Of course, you can feel a connection with a guy without spilling everything, but there will always be an expiration date on a relationship that lacks vulnerability. A connection that isn't standing on a strong enough foundation—with authenticity, trust, and vulnerability—can't stand the test of time. I learned this the hard way by being fearful of sharing my feelings in service to protecting myself, and through a lot of trial and error, I came to see that vulnerability is one of the greatest gifts you can give to yourself. Vulnerability is freedom; it's saying, "I am going to share how I feel no matter what because sharing my truth frees me from the shackles that I placed upon myself up until now."

Why are humans so afraid to share how they feel? Many of my clients have told me that sharing how they feel makes them feel completely naked. *OK, so what's so bad about that, especially if it's with someone you love?* (I can say this now that I'm on the other side; I know it's not easy to break through to vulnerability.) Let's change the lens of perception here. Being naked is a beautiful thing. Metaphorically speaking, it's stripping down to your vulnerable self. It's sharing your truth with another—and your truth is beautiful.

I know all that can sound terrifying if being vulnerable is not something you do, but I promise that once you start practicing, you will feel empowered.

NO ATTACHMENT TO THE OUTCOME

The first step in practicing vulnerability is to release your attachment to the outcome. Shift your perspective so that sharing how you feel is what matters more than how the guy reacts. His reaction is up to him. It is out of your control—and it has nothing do with you. I tell myself (and my clients) that being vulnerable is only scary if you make it scary. Instead of focusing on the fear, you can focus on the freedom! Sharing your truth with someone is a form of freedom.

One of the best stories I have of someone sharing their truth happened nearly half a century ago. The time were different, the devices didn't exist, but the courage of my Aunt Susie is timeless. She has inspired me, and her story continues to inspire my clients.

Susie and Arnie were on a date. It was 1970. They'd just graduated college, and Susie was set on moving to LA to pursue an acting career. Problem was, she'd have to leave Arnie and their relationship. All her friends were getting engaged, and she and Arnie had been together for a couple years and were friends for a million years before that. *What was he waiting for?* Susie started to wonder. (Yes, they were babies, but in the '70s getting married right after college was the norm.) Somewhere between the burgers and fries and the malted milkshake they shared for dessert, Susie popped the question.

"Arnie, I've been thinking about us a lot lately."

Gulp. Any twenty-two-year-old guy would be freaking out after his girlfriend starts a conversation like that. Of course, Arnie was in love with Susie too, but what now?

"And..." Susie was all nerves. "I mean, I love you so much. You're my dream man, and I know you love me..."

Arnie took another gulp.

"And we aren't getting any younger..." (OMG, they were babies! Did I already say that?)

"I love you too, Susie. You're my girl."

He's not getting it, Susie thought to herself.

"Well, I'm thinking of moving to Los Angeles to give acting a shot," she said, fumbling with the straw of their milkshake. "You know how much I love performing."

"And you're great at it," said Arnie. "Why can't you act here?"

"Well, I'd be happy to do my acting here in Chicago, but I would need a reason to stay."

"I'm here. Isn't that enough? And your family is here."

"You're not getting it. I mean a *real* reason. Something to bond us more than we are now. Something that would be worth not moving to LA for."

"So, what you're saying is your acting is more important than our relationship."

"No!" Susie yelled. "I'm saying that I want to be married! Why didn't you get that?"

"Ohhhhh." Arnie sat back in the booth. "Now I see what you're talking about."

He smiled at Susie.

"OK, Susie. So, let's get married."

"Are you asking me to marry you?" asked Susie, acting all coy.

"Yes. Susie Louise Gloria Leavitt, will you marry me?"

Aunt Susie and Uncle Arnie finished their milkshake, and the two lovebirds left the restaurant as an engaged couple that night, all thanks to Aunt Susie's vulnerability.

Although it doesn't appear that Susie MAN*ifested Arnie, she was clear on what she wanted, she trusted her intuition, she was willing to be vulnerable, and she went for it with no attachment to the outcome. Maybe she wasn't consciously MAN*ifesting when Uncle Arnie came into her life in high school, but her soul had been doing some major work behind the scenes to set it up so they could end up together. The Universe meets you at your point of action, and that woman acted on her desires. I have since crowned my Aunt Susie "Mrs. Magnificent MAN*ifester."

I, on the other hand, had a lot of work ahead of me. By the time Aunt Susie shared her story with me, I was deep in it— evolving, learning, growing, and I had yet to even get my toes wet in the practice of vulnerability. That experience would come with "The One Before The One."

Most women have an OBTO. I find it very common among my clients too. This is the man you become convinced is The One you will marry, only to find yourself devastated when the relationship ends.

JAIME, THE MR. UNAVAILABLE MAGNET

It was my second year out of college. I had just moved to New York and was living it up and working in the corporate arena of Estée Lauder in the famous General Motors Building in Midtown, right across from the Plaza Hotel. It was an entry-level job that had the potential to lead to product development and marketing. I felt cool. I was living it up in the Big Apple. Life was delicious and full of hope.

My roommates and I were at a bar when Ben walked in. He was mighty attractive and even more so when I talked with him. He had a soulful smile, and I had no trouble being the fun, confident, and playful girl I am. Since I was never one to have a boring conversation at a bar, I decided to share with Ben that I had been reading a palm-reading book and proceeded to read his palm. He thought it was pretty cool and that I was pretty witty. Meanwhile, I felt that I had escaped to paradise—because that's where holding his hand took me. I was bold with Ben.

"I have a feeling you are a Cancer," I said, still holding his hand.

"Yep," he said, looking into my soul.

He was impressed. I was loving the moment.

It was 1999, all the way back in the dark ages, right after the dinosaurs became extinct, before the age of all our convenient devices. This was back when you had to write your number down on a little piece of paper or give them your business card. That night no numbers were exchanged. *Had I misread his flirting?* I'm a pretty intuitive gal, so this was very surprising. I fell asleep that night, praying I would see him again.

I thought about Ben on and off for seven frustrating days.

The following weekend I was at a different bar with a different group of friends in a different part of the city. I was having a great time catching up with my college friends when I saw someone out of the corner of my eye. *No way. Not possible. How could that be* him? New York was one of the most populated cities on the planet. How could two people who didn't know each other end up at the same two bars two weekends in a row? Magic must be real.

Thank you, Universe, I thought as I walked over toward him.

That night we talked for hours. Ben was attentive, funny, clever, and for the first time in my life, I felt that a guy genuinely wanted to know everything about me. It was a feeling I had never experienced. "Wait. Tell me about YOU!" I said at one point when I realized that the whole conversation was about me. I wanted to know all about him. I was intrigued. He seemed wise beyond his years, an old soul, just how my friends always referred to me. We talked and laughed and closed down the bar at 2:00 a.m.

We did not exchange slips of paper or business cards. *Two amazing nights. Nothing?*

Back then, a person could dial 411 to get phone numbers from an operator. His last name was a bit unusual, so I found

Ben's number without a problem. With nervous anticipation, I dialed. His roommate picked up and took down my information. Ben called back within the hour, and we talked for hours. There was an undeniable comfort and familiarity. We had chemistry and an energetic connection.

"We should hang out sometime," I said.

I tried and failed to get my heart to stop the extra pounding.

"I have a girlfriend," he said. "She lives in Philadelphia."

I died inside. How was this true? We had just started to get to know one another. My heart hurt.

"Cool," I said, heartbreak and devastation taking over. "We can just be friends."

Rachel, from *Friends*, taught me to be this aloof.

After writing in my blue velvet journal one evening, I called my parents—my dad answered the phone—and I had to tell him I realized that I wanted to be vulnerable with a guy for the first time in my life. It was a strange yet sweet and refreshing feeling. Was I growing up? My heart felt open and bursting with joy. Before that, I didn't know what vulnerability was and why it was essential to practice. This was the tipping point. (Side note: The keyword is that I wanted to be vulnerable; was I? You'll have to continue reading to know that answer.)

"Where do you see yourself in five years? How many children do you imagine having?"

"What makes you happy? Do you have a good relationship with your mom?"

I was rattling off questions to Ben under the guise of a graduate school project.

I had started my graduate school program in psychology at New York University and would make up psychological tests and tell Ben it was part of my studies—creating an excuse to spend more time with him. I'd been in New York for almost two years, and Ben and I had been meeting up for dinner and drinks as if we were a couple prepping for a long-term relationship. Or we'd meet up at museum or he'd willingly watch me do karaoke. And if we didn't make plans, we'd always run into each other here and there, and I was certain The Universe had a reason to bring us together. Time didn't exist when I was with Ben. Life was more colorful, more magnificent. I was living in the flow. Everything was terrific about us—except that there wasn't really an "us," and we never even kissed. However, there was still a girl in Philly.

One night after a date-like dinner, as he walked me back to my apartment, we stopped by a place with a blinking neon sign that read: Psychic Readings Here. The psychic told us there was something about the color white that would be meaningful to us. A few days later, a white rose was taped to my front door.

A few weeks later, we were out together again, and as the night was winding down at a bar next to my building, he mentioned he had some news to tell me. He had gotten into Wharton at the University of Pennsylvania. My heart sank. I couldn't stop myself. I started crying. Philadelphia was just too many miles away from New York City.

He was shocked.

"If I had known how strongly you felt, I would have accepted the offer from Columbia and stayed in New York."

I was shocked that he was shocked!

My heart exited my body. I wanted someone to tell me that this wasn't happening. I was trying to be cool, but my insides were screaming. *No, please don't go! Stay here so we can continue this indescribable journey that we are on.* I wanted to say the words out loud, but I couldn't, so we both sat in our sadness and confusion.

That night he suggested we go to the rooftop, to see the city, something we would do sometimes. We stood there looking at the mesmerizing New York City lights together. It was cold. He turned me around to face him and enveloped me in his jacket. I loved the feeling of being close to him, close to his heart and held tightly in his arms. I looked up at him, he looked back at me, and then he kissed me! You know when you want something so much that you feel like it's never going to happen? After a year and a half of knowing him, it finally happened. It was a glimpse into what heaven would feel like. My whole mind, body, and spirit were euphoric. That kiss was one of the best moments of my life.

The next day I was floating.

I needed an excuse to talk to him, so I sent him an email. It was just something simple, a reference to an inside joke between us.

I shouldn't have done that. He's not going to write back because he was freaked out by last night. He will see right through my lame excuse to contact him.

He wrote back twenty-seven minutes later.

"I'm happy you're studying to be a therapist because I will need one after last night. You gave me a lot to think about and some clarity."

He was on a break from the Philly girl, so maybe he'd never be going back to her! I was on cloud nine. Mission accomplished! I had gotten his wheels to spin, to realize that there was much more potential in "us." A kiss can do that, you know—it's one of the ways that I encourage my clients to know how they feel about a guy.

"So, what happens now, Jaime?"

Ben brushed a piece of my hair behind my ear. Beautiful feels jetted through my body.

He had come over to my apartment to celebrate his birthday—and his move to Wharton. I made him cupcakes and looked cute in white capris and a white tank. (We were all about white, remember?)

"You know I'm dating Andrew, right?" Andrew was sweet and fun, but he was no Ben in my book. But Ben was moving so…"And you have your situation in Philly. [I didn't know what their status was, and I didn't ask.] So, we'll have to see what happens."

I was trying to play it cool, but this is what I really wanted to say:

What happens now, Ben? In my world, what happens now is that you tell me how you honestly feel about me, and I tell you how I honestly feel about you. We tell each other that we love each other and don't want to live without each other, and then we decide that we should be together and live happily ever after…somewhere between New York City and Philly.

If I had the strength of heart—the feminine courage—that I have now, that's how it would have gone down. But I didn't. I didn't know how to be vulnerable. I didn't have what my Aunt Susie had. We had another unbelievable kiss, but that was that.

In March, he sent me my favorite flowers for my birthday. I was floored, elated, beyond happy, jumping up and down, dancing around my apartment. I called and thanked him. I don't think he will ever realize how much joy those flowers brought to my heart.

When I finished grad school, I moved to LA. Ben and I kept in touch, even saw each other once after moving. The following spring, he was graduating from Wharton. One day I received an email.

"We will be moving to Dallas after grad school."

Ben had a little aquarium with a fish named Sammy. I emailed back.

"You and Sammy are moving to Dallas? That's great!"

He responded hours later.

"No, me and Philly."

My heart hurt.

Whoa, this is over. I never thought that that day would come. I thought that we would end up together. When you have a soul connection with someone, it's not something that happens daily. After that, I stewed on it for a long time, and then I finally emailed him—the longest email I'd ever written. It took hours to write, words and words just flowing out of me. I felt that if it was going to be over between us, I needed him to know how I truly felt about him. I shared everything about what my journey felt like with him. I told him that I had fallen in love with him. I was as vulnerable as a human could possibly be. I was surprised that I had no fear. Intuitively, I knew it had to be said, and I wanted him to know.

Sending that email was my first glimpse into what it feels like to live an authentic life, which I do now. Back then, I was younger, and I didn't yet know the empowerment that comes from being vulnerable. When you say what you need to say, from your heart, you can never go wrong. It's the best thing you can do in life. The people who are supposed to be in your life will hear you and want to be in your life.

So, the mature man that he was, Ben picked up the phone and called me. He told me that I was amazing and that he knew that I was going to find an amazing guy. I thanked him. It was a brief conversation because there was nothing else to talk about. We said goodbye, and our saga was over. I didn't cry, which was shocking. Instead, I felt little lighter, as if maybe I could move on. Finally! I could live my life without that unknown that was always hanging over our relationship. I now knew—he wasn't The One.

But as the days went on, I became increasingly sad as I reflected on everything. I missed him. I couldn't believe that something with so much potential was just done. Gone. Vanished. I was frustrated that I never got to hear how he truly felt about me. I knew he had feelings for me, but I never got to hear it. I played it over one night in my head again and again, beating myself up for not snacking before I washed my face.

We had had dinner and said goodnight. I returned to my apartment and was washing my face when I saw that he had called me. I called him right back and asked him why he called. "Oh, it was nothing," he said. "Never mind." He was lying. He wanted to tell me something and then just didn't. It wasn't fair. I was mad at myself for washing my face right away because I usually have a snack when I get home and then wash my face. *Why did I have to wash my face?* I went over it again and again.

Now I know better about Ben. It couldn't have happened any other way, and that's what I want to teach you. I know what it feels like to look back and wish that something would have turned out differently, and I stopped doing that years ago when I learned that everything truly happens precisely how it is supposed to, in alignment with your soul's journey. As much as it hurts in the moment, it is the right thing happening at the right time.

One day, you will look back and think to yourself, *Oh, that's why so-and-so didn't work. It all makes sense now.* I was supposed to wash my face. He was supposed to go to Wharton. That's the whole point of my story, the whole energy around the OBTO. You *think* he had to be it, because he was so easy to see as The One.

We can, and we must, learn something from every relationship, keeping in mind the knowledge that it couldn't have happened any other way. I am now aware that I wasn't supposed to be as open with my feelings for Ben. I was doing the best that I could at the time, but after reading this book and learning about vulnerability, I encourage you to learn from me. When you do feel strongly for a man, do yourself a favor and tell him (not on the first date, but after you have something established). Tell him because that's a weight off your soul. But tell him and do not try to predict the outcome. Share your truest feelings and then get out of your own way. Let The Universe bring you closer to The One.

Everything is meant to be, and timing is everything. If that saga hadn't ended, I would have never met my sweetheart husband, Bryan.

I was being The Mr. Unavailable Magnet. This persona is drawn to guys that aren't on the market. This is convenient because being in love with someone who is taken protects us from ever having a real relationship. Sure, I dated other guys during those five years, but they were "time-passer-byers," as I like to call them. From my perspective and my heart, Ben was always my man. I couldn't see—and would not let myself have—as strong of a connection with another man. Instead, I wasted so much time and energy on something that never really was.

Being The Mr. Unavailable Magnet taught me some important lessons. I learned the cost of holding back and pretending that I was OK being lovers one moment and friends the next. I had to learn to open up and be honest with myself and others if I was ever going to find my true "Mr. Right." Being The Mr. Unavailable Magnet also taught me to use my voice. If you have something to say in life, you need to say it. I can promise you that you will regret *not* taking the risk and telling a man how you feel more than whatever happens if you take the risk. You are not the Little Mermaid. No one has taken your voice away. You were given a beautiful voice to use, so you need to use it. Finding my voice has been one of the most empowering experiences of my life thus far.

I used my voice when I was dating my husband, and I use it in our marriage. I remember on our fourth date I told Bryan how every date I went on with him I started to like him more and more. (I also remember being shocked that I was sharing my heart and speaking up like that.) And now, in our marriage, when I have a compliment to give him, a sentiment I want to share or something bothering me, I share it with him. I share it with him and with no attachment to the outcome.

It's time to overcome your fear of how the guy is going to respond and realize that it's more important that you honor yourself by speaking from your heart. That is freedom. Don't hold yourself back anymore. The world, especially your man, needs to hear what you say.

CHAPTER SEVEN EXERCISE: BE VULNERABLE

This exercise will push you out of your comfort zone in a big way. The risk is worth the reward. In being vulnerable, you will emerge empowered.

#1: Think of a guy you dated—this can be an ex-boyfriend or a guy you casually dated but always wanted to turn into something else. Whoever you choose, it needs to be a man you feel you never really expressed your true feelings for because you held yourself back. Someone with whom you never shared the facts about what your heart was feeling because you were protecting it.

#2: Take out a pen and paper and write this man a heartfelt letter. Be as open and honest as humanly possible in this letter. Sharing this with him will set you free. It will set you free from wondering what could have been. It will set you free from living in the past. You are going to put it all on the table. (I know, it's terrifying!) Share how you felt (or feel) about him with no attachment to the outcome. This isn't about him— it's about YOU, my friend, and your freedom and peace. You are setting yourself free from the burden of regret as you show The Universe that you're not hiding or playing small anymore when it comes to attracting The One.

#3: It's not necessary to send the letter to your man. You can but know that it's the act of writing it that provides real healing.

Even if he never sees the letter or hears your words, know that you are putting your feelings out there and that will be the release and a healing that you need. It will free up space in your consciousness and heart for The One to come in. Regret can take up a lot of room and consume energy, so releasing it is beyond transformative.

If you'd prefer to do this verbally, by all means, call the guy up or ask to see him in person. It doesn't matter how you communicate your message. All that matters is that you DO express your message.

CHAPTER EIGHT

Going into the Field

Affirmation: "Nothing is in the way of me and the man I came to this earth to be with. I am in the flow and ready to fly. I am surrendering to The Universe: I fully trust in you, and I know that you will bring into my life exactly what I need at exactly the right time."

YOU ARE HUMAN, AS you know, and now you also know that you are a divine being having a human experience. Your life has played out exactly the way it was supposed to and will continue to—everything in divine timing. Here you are today, a stronger and wiser woman ready to take on the world.

Let's celebrate how far you've come. Unconditional self-love, and living life for your authentic self, is your jam now, and you better believe it's a sexy jam! This is it. There's no turning back. You've lived your life holding yourself back for way too long. You have now seen that holding on to your old personas is like carrying around a one-thousand-pound weight. You have looked at anything that needed healing, anything that was unresolved, and now you have the freedom to let it all go.

You've cultivated confidence, done the exercises, repeated your affirmations, written in your journal, laughed and cried, and maybe had a few Ben & Jerry's and *When Harry Met Sally* nights on the couch. After all, no one said that growing pains are easy, but I applaud you for letting out all those tears. You needed it, and tears are beautiful.

This book has given you the means to identify when your fear-based dating persona tries to creep in and run the show as well as the tools to take back your power and reconnect to your authentic self. You are the boss of you. You are the expert on you. You know that you've been the only thing holding you back from your man. So now that you are out of your way, all that's left to do is be present, believe that it's going to happen for you, and make that conscious effort to show up in life as your authentic self and NOTHING less. You know that you deserve the world. You are meant to have that love that is waiting for you.

You have earned your superwoman cape, and you're ready to fly. Suppose you happen to fly into a red flag or two on the way; no need to freak out because now you know how to spot them and fly the other way. The old you would've been stuck on that date or in that relationship for hours, days, or years too long, but not anymore. You know who you are, you know what you want, and nothing is in the way of you and your man. You also understand that once you find him, you're not going to have a tight grip; you're going to trust yourself, The Universe, and the relationship that it will unfold exactly how it is supposed to. All you need to do is show up as you and enjoy the ride.

Control and fear of the unknown are a thing of the past. Trust and surrender are your new besties. Your lens of perception has shifted, and you're showing up standing strong in your integrity. People in your life will notice something is different, but they won't know exactly what it is. You're glowing from the inside out, and your energy is illuminating.

Your light is shining bright, and you know now that it never went anywhere; it was just temporarily dimmed. You are not playing small and hiding anymore. The world, especially your man, wants to see you, know you, and be around you. You are electrifying.

You are fiercely fearless in pursuing your birthright to love and be loved. You will be united with your "person," your man, whom you've been waiting for your whole life. You are done with living a fear-based life. All that's left to do is attack the world (you know what I mean); you are attacking life because you feel alive again.

You are that person who lights up a room.

You are the one who people want to be around.

You are the one who ignites the fire. Speaking of fire, that fire that is waiting to be lit by your guy—that fire will never go out because now you know better. There are no more regrets, settling, or making decisions based on anything else but what your heart needs and says, "YES!" to.

Throughout reading this book, you have already experienced some synchronicities in your life. As you continue with your MAN*ifesting journey, you will continue to experience beautiful, eye-opening, and magical validations that you are on the right track. You have been in your man's orbit, and he has been in yours, and soon enough, your orbits will be intertwined. Please let me know when you meet him!

The MAN*ifesting journey you've been on will all be worth it, trust me—or rather, trust yourself because you know how to now.

You are the co-creator of your life. LOVE life, and it will all be incredible.

I acknowledge you and commend you for investing in yourself. The knowledge and wisdom you now have are not to be taken lightly. This book was not meant to come into your life only for you to go back to your old ways. This book is meant to transform your life. You know better now. Any fear, negative thought, or feeling that surfaces, just allow it and know that "you've got this." Once you learn something, you can't unlearn it—and if you've read the words and practiced the exercises, then you've learned something in this book. You have evolved and leveled up your life and love game. Now it's time to put it all into practice. I call this "going out into the field."

TAKING ACTION

"I'm going out into the field tonight, as you like to say, Jaime!"

My clients say things like this to me all the time once they've reached this stage, and it never gets old hearing it! But before they experience this kind of confidence, they often ask, "What now?" You might be asking the very same question. You've done the work to meet The One on the inside, but what about meeting The One in the outside world, the world you greet as soon as you walk out of your home? The world of dating?

This chapter is where I offer practical guidelines to consider when you are dating. I'm giving you dating cheat sheets! Return to them anytime you feel you've veered off track or that you are falling back into old fear-based, inauthentic, or negative patterns.

THE FIRST DATE CHEAT SHEET

#1: Be Present

When you're on the date, make sure that you are there with him and not in your head wondering if he likes you, does your hair look OK, or what will our wedding be like. When you are vibing with a guy, instead of fixating and praying that he feels the same way about you, keep the focus on how you're feeling in the moment and enjoy it. Being present allows for you to show up as your authentic self. And don't kid yourself, when you're in your head on a date the guy can sense it. It's not attractive. Imagine being on a date with a guy constantly on his phone. You wouldn't like that. Be present. Get out of your head, and I hope I don't have to tell you to put the phone down.

#2: Be Selfish

Dating is an investment of your time and energy, so do your best to enjoy it as much as possible. You do not want to resent dating. If every date is two hours, you won't want to go or dating will become more like work. This is your time, and if you know that forty-five minutes over coffee or a dog walk is good for the first get-to-know-you, then stick to it. And if you're on a date and you know it's a "no," then respect that "knowing" and make it as short as it needs to be.

#3: Be Lighthearted and Have FUN

Keep the conversation light. Yes, I wrote a whole chapter about being vulnerable, but remember how I said, "Not on the first date!" I meant that. I'm all about being vulnerable, but that doesn't mean exposing your deepest and darkest secrets at the beginning of a relationship. In the beginning, have as much fun as possible and enjoy each other's presence. Get to know all the good stuff about each other and share in the things you love to do. When the time is right you will know when to let it all pour out.

#4: No Negative Ex Talking

Do not bring up your ex. Although the subject may come up organically, such as when your date asks why you broke up, all you need to say is, "We just weren't right for one another." That's the end of the story. You do not need to talk about your ex, and you definitely do not need to talk negatively about your ex. Eventually, if and when this date turns into more dates, yes, disclose whatever you'd like to, but not while you are still building a foundation. You don't want any of that negative energy lingering in the air, invading your new space with a new man. Imagine, you tell a guy that your last boyfriend cheated on you. This leaves space for the guy to start to wonder why, and that interrupts the flow of you getting to know each other for who you are rather than you now being a victim of infidelity.

#5: No Attachment to the Outcome

Before you go on a date, set an intention that no matter what the outcome is, you trust that it is supposed to happen. Try to stay as neutral as possible, because then you won't be disappointed if it doesn't work out, you will just be happy if it does. In fact, revisit the exercise from chapter 4 where you let The Universe know that you are open to what it has in store for you.

My whole life has been a study of love. I've always been fascinated by it, and I couldn't end this book without sharing one of the most incredible models of love I've ever experienced. I'd go so far as to say that I do what I do because I need the world to know that true love exists. My love for love all started from a very early age because I had the honor of watching my parents adore each other, and I continue to witness this.

My parents just celebrated fifty-one years of marriage, and I see them as the epitome of what a soul-connected, happy, healthy, and forever marriage can look like. Maybe they can be an inspiration for you too. Whether it was my dad dancing with my mom, twirling her around and dipping her in the middle of the kitchen while she was cooking dinner, or how they to this day look at each other and smile from their soul, I have always felt such joy watching them. I light up when I am in their presence, and I know that I am experiencing their love. Once in a while, I get a peek at the cards they write to each other. Their cards are usually not long, but their words are powerful and poignant. Their love isn't cheesy or overdone. Their love is understated, authentic, and genuine.

My parents rarely fight. Rarely, not never because they are human. In fact, the ability to be in conflict with another is a sign of a deep connection—you have to care about someone enough to fight. When it comes to my parents, I wouldn't even call them fights. Frustrations would be a better description. When my mom is angry with my dad, my dad serenades her with the lyrics to "Sue Me," a song from the musical *Guys and Dolls*. In his endearing way, he mimics the song by telling my mom to call a lawyer and sue him for not helping with the laundry (or whatever it was that was bothering my mom).

He sings it in an adorable way that naturally forces my mom to melt and laugh at the endearing gesture. This doesn't mean that my dad gets away with whatever it was that bothered my mom. She always tells him how she is feeling, and then my dad usually tells her he had no idea she was upset and then he apologizes and sings, and she cracks up. In many ways the song is a redirection and a reminder of how much my dad cherishes my mom, and her receiving the gesture with a smile, an embrace, and sometimes a dance shows my dad how much she appreciates him trying to make her happy—and succeeding.

My parents' relationship is fun. They travel and go to new places. While growing up, I remember them going on a lot of dates and being out and about with other couples. I would get sad sometimes because I liked it better when they were around, but I understand now that nurturing and tending to their relationship and bond was and is so important. To this day, my parents keep up their social life and are always discovering places to go.

My mom always says that it was dumb luck that they worked out because they were so young when they fell in love and got married, but from my perspective—from a personal and professional point of view—I see two people who came to this earth to be together and found each other. Their love is infectious. They are modest, never boastful, and always grateful for what they have with zero reason to show it off. They know their worth, their gifts, their hearts, and their connection, and they know that's all that matters. I, too, am beyond grateful to have been given the gift of witnessing what real love and a happy marriage can look like.

As you continue your MAN*ifesting journey, remember to be patient. Not all great loves find each other fast. Some take time, but now that you have all the tools, you can feel excited about what is coming. Don't get discouraged if the first date out of the gate isn't The One—or if you discover that after twenty great dates in. You are getting closer to The One every day and every date. Eventually, when you find yourself in a fully committed relationship, and you want to make sure that this really could be your forever, go through the following checklist to see if you have at least most of the items on the list to verify that he really could be your "person."

#1: You can be your authentic self with him.

#2: You can't get enough of him.

#3: You are intrigued by him.

#4: You miss him when one of you is traveling.

#5: He feels like HOME.

#6: You can't imagine being with anyone else.

#7: He is your favorite person.

#8: You feel safe with him (especially when you're enveloped in his arms).

COULD HE BE THE ONE?

Assess the following qualities so that you feel confident about potentially marrying this man.

#1: Grow and THRIVE, not Survive

The two people in the relationship have to do more than survive for the relationship to thrive. A relationship will not be sustainable if only one person is working on themselves and growing as an individual. Both people need to be willing to grow individually if the relationship will grow. If no one wants to live their best life possible for each other, the relationship won't last. If only one person does, the couple won't be in sync.

It's unattractive to look at someone and see that they don't respect themselves enough to take care of themselves, all the while knowing they are capable of much more than they are giving themselves credit for. Or when one person tries to inspire the other one to help them see their worth and value, but to no avail, it is daunting and detrimental to the mental and emotional health of the individuals and the couple. However, when there are two people who desire to live their best possible lives and work to grow, learn, and live, then their relationship will naturally grow and evolve with them.

#2: Share New Experiences Together

Having variety in life is important. Eating the same salad for lunch every day or consistently taking the same route to the grocery store can prohibit the brain from getting the exercise it needs, and it's just plain dull. The same goes for relationships. Having new experiences together is essential. Doing a new activity or trying out a new restaurant occasionally is healthy, exciting, stimulating, and fun.

New experiences are moments of bonding that create history and memories while strengthening the connection between the two individuals. When a couple tries something new together and has a novel experience, those feel-good endorphins like serotonin and dopamine start firing. Fun fact about increased dopamine: it increases your testosterone, which increases sexual desire, so having some extra dopamine around can enhance your sex life also. New ventures are uplifting, and being uplifted together feels invigorating.

#3: *Have a Deep Emotional Connection*

A forever relationship is not surface level. You can love anyone, but when you feel a deep emotional connection, you feel at home. Being with this person feels "right" and "completely comfortable." *When you know, you know* is what I'm talking about here. Couples who are each other's The One revealed that their significant other "feels like home." It's a familiarity and warmth, something that goes far beyond looking good on paper. They are two people who fit together mind, body, and soul.

#4: *No Judgment*

You want to marry someone whom you accept without any judgment. When we judge someone, we can't connect with that person, which is why any bit of judgment makes it difficult to have a relationship.

The less judging you do, the more you can connect and start accepting one another for who you are. Of course, there might be little things that people can change, like a smoking habit, but the core of a person—their soul—doesn't change. I know so many people who get married and think their spouse will change when they're officially together, and then they get disappointed when it doesn't happen. Know, accept, and love whom you are marrying before you get married.

#5: *Vulnerability*

Just as judgment snuffs out connection, vulnerability sparks it. When we share ourselves fully, we subconsciously give the other person in the relationship permission to share themselves fully. There is no better feeling than when we are free to be who we are and feel adored, accepted, and understood. Vulnerability is a strength that leads to freedom, the freedom to be completely who we are in our rawest form. Freedom to be naked.

#6: Have Fun and LAUGH

Fun is a fundamental part of a forever relationship. My mom always talks about how it's essential to find someone to play with in life, and I couldn't agree more. As a student of love, I have interviewed "thriving" couples throughout the years as I explore the common threads of what makes couples last. The couples all talk a lot about how they enjoy life together and have fun. However, you can't look to other couples to see what they are doing to have fun, because fun is subjective. Whatever having fun means to each couple is suitable only for that couple.

When you are looking to discover what is fun, don't look at what you are doing. Look at how you are doing and what you are feeling. What gives you the ability to lighten up, laugh, and enjoy each other's company? You will soon find things you love to do together that will make life more fun.

#7: Compassionate Conflict Resolution

Couples who fight well together stay together. It is normal for couples to fight, but how you fight determines the longevity and strength of a relationship. Couples who value and respect one another have a much easier time working through conflict than couples with no regard for each other's feelings. I always tell my clients who are struggling in their relationships that they should start the conversation by saying "I love you" to one another. This will foster connection and break down any walls that are up. Saying those three meaningful words can be disarming to speak or hear, but it helps one person to tune in and listen to the other person's feelings, which is crucial to conflict resolution.

Telling someone you love them is one thing, but telling someone they should or shouldn't feel a certain way is another. Dictating feelings is not conducive to a healthy relationship. We all want to feel seen and heard in relationships and life, and it is the couples who can see and hear each other that know how to handle conflict.

One of the leading experts in the field of relationships is Dr. John Gottman of the Gottman Institute. He figured out a way to predict the longevity of a marriage. Through his research studies, he discovered that the difference between happy and unhappy couples is how they balance positive and negative interactions while working on resolving their conflicts. This means that when he saw lightheartedness, compassion, and even humor as couples tried to resolve an issue, he saw that as a determiner of relationship success. I couldn't agree more!

#8: You're Best Friends and Each Other's "Person"

"I choose to marry DJ because he's my best friend. He's my favorite person," to quote my friend Jen.

Couples who describe each other as best friends would choose their spouse over anyone else in the world to spend their life with. There is an unspoken bond, connection, and understanding between them—a tie that gets stronger as time passes. The energy that exists between these couples is palpable, and the depths of the love they feel for each other are breathtaking.

LIFE IS OUR TEACHER

I have learned A LOT about relationships in my life. I was a romantic when I was younger, and I still am, but I don't romanticize love (or energy) anymore. I have seen that life is not perfect, it can be messy at times, but it also is beautiful, and the most crucial part is finding someone with whom you can enjoy the journey of life.

Life happens for you, not to you. Therein lies the opportunity to see growth, learning lessons, and a potential to discover more about how you are and how you can show up in every relationship as authentically as possible. Not all dates turn into true love, as we know. However, some of them do, and your time will happen sooner rather than later if you are open to it and all that you can learn about yourself along the way. When The One arrives, you will be in heaven, relishing in the glory and joy of the relationship. That's the beginning. It's what comes after the honeymoon period that counts.

Once you've been dating for a while, some soul-searching will need to occur before you know for sure if this is The One. You will be asked to discern between knowing if it's authentic love or your ego forcing it to be. If it's not real between the two of you—despite what other people may think—you know it is time to move on. You will only be wasting your time and your man's time, spending time away from the person with whom each of you is respectively supposed to be. Trust that little gnawing feeling in the back of your mind. Take a closer look. Be honest with yourself. Ask yourself these questions:

#1: Can you genuinely see yourself being with this man for the rest of your life?

#2: Do you feel deep down in your gut—in your bones—
that you have found your "person," the one who came to
this earth for you?

#3: Do you adore him with your whole heart?

#4: Do you like him?

People surprise themselves when they realize
they love the guy, but they don't like him. Oh, that's a
RED FLAG!

#5: Do you feel you are compatible in life, love, humor, and
serious times?

#6: Are you emotional equals? You've heard of "emo-
tional intelligence." In a relationship, you want to be
on the same page as your man. Without equal levels
of emotional intelligence, a relationship will remain
surface and high levels of resentment and frustration
are usually experienced. Some examples of emotional
intelligence are:

– Being able to share how you're feeling
– Being able to own up and not blame
– Being able to be resilient and forgive

#7: Do you feel that your love is strong enough to get
through anything?

"Jaime, make sure that you are over the moon for the guy
because in a marriage there are a lot of moons to go over."

Wise words from my mom, which at the time felt a bit
shocking coming from her, the woman who was entirely in
love with—and in like with—my dad. Shocking, but refreshing,
because that showed me that their marriage wasn't as perfect
as I had thought it was. Because nothing lasting is perfect. My

mom's point is that if you are genuinely in love, then you can get through any hurdle and you get through it together. I've since learned from my own marriage that nothing is perfect and that getting through tough times can strengthen you as a couple.

I'm not a fan of comparison; however, it can be helpful to have a model of an ideal relationship for inspirational purposes. Think back to some weddings you've attended, where you could viscerally feel the love between the couple standing at the altar. You had no doubt they would last—these two were meant to be together. As you watched the bride and groom profess their love to each other in their speeches, what are some of the things you heard?

"I can't get enough of you."

"I want to grow old with you."

"I can't imagine spending the rest of my life with anyone else."

"You inspire me."

These aren't just cheesy lines that people repeat because they have nothing better to say. These lines have been exchanged throughout history between couples who are supposed to be together, because they are saying exactly what they mean from the center of their hearts. And when two people really mean what they say, the simplest of sayings is magical.

When you get to the point where you feel that you have found The One, can you imagine saying lines like that to him and him saying them back to you? Does it make you emotional? Well then, my dear, you have found your "forever." Mazel tov! However, if you have ANY doubts, the answer is "no." If you are making excuses as to why you should get married or if it doesn't feel right in your heart, then he is not The One for you.

This is your life, and if you want to avoid going your separate ways in the future, I want to save you from entering into a marriage where, ultimately, you are not happy. I don't care if you are fifty…or eighty and haven't gotten married yet. There should never be a rush on The One. When you know you've found The One, it will be the most beautiful, joyful, and love-filled "yes" you will ever feel.

CHAPTER EIGHT EXERCISE: BE COURAGEOUS

#1: *At the top of your MAN*ifesting journal page, write: "Now that I am entirely courageous, then what?"*

For example:

- *"Now that I am entirely courageous, nothing is in my way of manifesting my man."*
- *"Now that I am entirely courageous, I am free from myself."*
- *"Now that I am entirely courageous, I know I am fully healed and untethered to the past."*
- *"Now that I am entirely courageous, I don't have anything holding me back from moving forward."*

#2: *After you write your statements, follow them up with this line:*

"Now that I am entirely courageous, all of my dreams are coming true."
And for the first time in your life, you will believe it!

#3: *Now, go out there and BE courageous. Feel courage in your heart, breathe courage, DO courage.*

Get out of your comfort zone and take a risk. For example:

- *Text a guy you've been scared to text.*
- *Say "yes" to invitations you wouldn't usually say "yes" to.*
- *Go to an event or party by yourself if you can't find anyone to go with you.*

- *Walk up to a handsome man in a bar or a restaurant and say "Hi."*

Live your life with the mentality that you have nothing to lose because the truth is you have nothing to lose, and when you take chances, you have everything to gain.

When being courageous, you shift your energy and invite in newness. Being courageous reminds you of what you are capable of. Your power has always been within, it was just a matter of getting past the barriers that have held you back in the past...but not anymore. Courage is your new middle name. All you need to do is to give yourself permission to shine.

Your love won't come into your world if you operate at low-energy or low-vibration levels. One way to be courageous and step out of your comfort zone to raise your vibration is to do things you don't normally do. Every time you change it up, so to speak, you increase your vibration a little more.

Be the ignited light. Take the fire within and run with it. What started as just a spark is now unstoppable. Your momentum will continue to set your soul on fire.

You are stepping into the rest of your life, so hold on because it's about to get a lot better!

Consider yourself courageous. You are ready to go out into the field. You are ready for The Universe to send you The One. Look in the mirror each morning and say to yourself, "Now that I am entirely courageous..." (you finish the sentence):

> *"...nothing is in my way of manifesting my man."*
> *"...I am free from myself."*
> *"...I know I am fully healed and untethered to the past."*
> *"...all of my dreams are coming true."*
>
> *Go out there and get your man. You've never been closer to manifesting all that you have desired. You're ready. The moment you close this book, you are stepping into the rest of your life. Get excited, because it's about to get a lot better!*

Years ago, I was walking on the beach in Hawaii with my dad (my first prince), and I was beyond distraught over what to do about the Ben situation. My heart and head were telling me different messages, and I needed some sound advice. My dad, who is a numbers guy, provided me with a mathematical and statistical answer...not quite what I expected, but I loved hearing anything he had to offer. He laid out four different action steps that would yield four different outcomes. He used his finger to draw the four action steps in the air as if he were drawing on a chalkboard—oh how I love my dad. The four options were as follows:

1. I could tell him how I feel.
2. I could find another man.
3. I could end things with Ben.
4. I could continue in the limbo state that the relationship was in.

My dad asked me to think of it as a "chi-square." (I'd never heard of one of those, but he explained it was a math term.) I started crying. I felt lost and scared.

I thought about each action step, and after feeling completely overwhelmed, a surge of courage washed over me. I knew that I needed to take some sort of action when I returned home. I didn't know how it would look but knew I needed to do something. I was ready, and the love and support I felt from my dad, my rock, helped me to be courageous.

When it comes to taking chances, my dad said it best. "Jaime, there are no guarantees in life, so you need to take a chance and go for it." He couldn't have been more right about that. And I'd like to add to that brilliant quote: If it doesn't work out, trust that there's a reason. You're always being protected by The Universe. But nothing will happen if you don't take action. Unbeknownst to me, that was the beginning of my MAN*ifesting journey. And now you are on yours, fully equipped with an open heart. You know you're ready, The Universe knows you're ready, and soon enough you will be in the arms of your man. You'll be beyond grateful and elated, with a full heart, smiling, knowing that you invested in yourself and you took a chance on love.

You're ready. Now go and MAN*ifest your destiny!

BONUS EXERCISE: REFLECTION AND INTROSPECTION

In life and love, I have found that one of the most helpful things I have done is to reflect on my life and what I have learned. So, I'm going to ask you to do just that as you near the end of this journey.

*#1: Think back on your MAN*ifesting journey thus far. Take a moment right now, close your eyes, and take five deep breaths. Have your MAN*ifesting journal ready, and then return to this page.*

#2: Write down the following prompts and then answer them. Let the answers come to you with no force, just allow the words to flow.

- *What is the most eye-opening, surprising lesson that stands out to you?*
- *What have you learned about yourself?*
- *What have you learned about love and relationships?*
- *What has inspired you the most?*
- *What has brought you to tears (the good tears—breakthrough tears)?*
- *What are your action steps?*

It's important to reflect and remind ourselves of what we've learned because it helps us be prepared to take action steps.

- *What will you do differently now that you know what you know?*
- *How are you going to show up?*
- *What will you not settle for anymore?*

- *In a year from now_____ (complete the sentence).*
- *In five years from now_____ (complete the sentence).*
- *In ten years from now _____ (complete the sentence).*

#3: As you continue your MAN*ifesting journey, from time to time, look back at how you answered these questions. It will be a perfect reference point to keep you on track and also see what transpires along the way. It will also be fascinating to see where you are in your evolution compared to where you began.

ACKNOWLEDGMENTS

WRITING *MAN*IFESTING* HAS BEEN a journey and a labor of love. I have put my heart into every minute, hour, word on the page, sentiment, and inspirational message. As hard as I have worked, I would not have been able to get to this place without some very integral and special people. They say it takes a village, and that statement could not be more accurate! I am beyond grateful for my village, the people who see me, know me, support me, and love me unconditionally as I do them tenfold. My team is made up of people from all areas of my life, and they are all unique in their own ways, but the one thing they have in common is heart; they care about the world and being good people. Those are the people that have enriched my life tremendously.

To my parents, thank you for bringing me into this world and naming me "Jaime." "J'aime" means "I love" in French. I am grateful that I was destined to dedicate my life and work to love, all the beautiful aspects it brings to my life, and all the love I am honored to share. Thank you for your endless unconditional love and support and for all the wisdom you have imparted to me. I cherish every moment I spend with both of you. Thank you for believing in me and my dreams and for loving each other the way you do. It truly is an honor to see the joy in your faces when you look at one another. Your love and admiration are beyond inspirational.

To my husband, Bryan, thank you for your support, loving me, knowing me, and seeing me for all I am. It means a lot! I appreciate you being there for me during those times of overwhelm. You patiently listened and always helped me get back to a place of staying on track as I reminded myself of my eternal goal of changing lives for the better. The work that goes into the creative process of birthing a book is sacred and not for the faint of heart; thank you for honoring that. And thank you for being an amazing dad to Noah.

To Noah, thank you for being the old soul that you are. Sometimes you say the wisest things that are so sweet and helpful; you always know what I need to hear at the moment. And thank you for being my manager and promoting my work to everyone we meet by saying, "You know, my mom is 'The Relationship Expert!' She can help you!" You are an angel, and you crack me up with your randomness and wittiness.

To my brothers, Michael and Scott, I am so grateful for both of you, and I love being in the middle and protected in my sibling sandwich. I love that you will always be there for me, and I appreciate your love for my family and me; also, you are the best uncles!

Thank you so much to my sister (in-law), Liza. You are definitely the sister I never had but always wanted to have! Your friendship means so much to me. Thank you for always being there for me. The fun times and laughs we've had are countless. I'm so happy that you met Scott and became part of our family!

Thank you to my grandma, Esther; you were such a pivotal part of being there for me on my "MAN*ifesting" journey. Your love is palpable. You have the biggest heart, and I thank you for passing down your love genes. We love *big*, and we feel *big*! I'm eternally grateful for your pure unconditional love and support.

To my friends who have been there for me along this book journey and in life in general! I appreciate your support, help with the creative process, and most of all, your friendship, (in alphabetical order) Abby, Ally, Andrea, Gwen, Jenna, Kristin, Jackie, Leslie, Lori, Robin, Robyn, Maggie, and Sydney.

Thank you to my clients for inviting me to witness your healing, evolving, learning, and growing; it's a true honor. Your dedication to living your best life possible is remarkable.

Thank you to Drs. Ron and Mary Hulnick. There are truly no words to describe how you've enhanced my life. You are two of the most extraordinary humans on this planet. The education I received from you is priceless, life-changing, and magical. You up-leveled my life and deepened my personal work and my life's work.

Thank you to Anthony Ziccardi at Post Hill Press for believing in me and my vision for my book. Thank you to Madeline Sturgeon, the managing editor, who was so patient and helpful every step of the way! Thank you to Ja Racharaks for editing my book so thoroughly. You were born to be an editor. Your thoughtful feedback after reading my manuscript validated that I accomplished the messages and teachings I strived to portray.

To my assistant, Jennifer Gellman, and my designer, Kaitlyn Rodenbucher; thank you for your patience and endless creativity.

To the editors who helped with my book proposal and pre-manuscript, Janna Hockenjos, Cindy Ditiberio, and Richelle Fredson, thank you for being such pivotal parts of my book journey. All of you were so instrumental in helping to piece together *MAN*ifesting*.

Thank you so much to the PR team at Sarah Hall Productions and at Post Hill Press for spreading the word about *MAN*ifesting*. I am so thankful for all of your efforts on my behalf. I aim to inspire and change as many lives as possible, and you are helping to make that happen!

To Maria Vowteras and Johnny Russo, someone up there orchestrated our meeting, and I am so grateful as you two are the definition of a dynamic duo!

ABOUT THE AUTHOR

PHOTO BY PAUL WESTLAKE

JAIME BRONSTEIN, LCSW, is a relationship coach, author, speaker, and host of *Love Talk Live* on LA Talk Radio. Jaime has shared her relationship advice on various media outlets such as ABC, NBC, CBS, KTLA News, Forbes, *The New York Times*, USA Today, *People Magazine*, and Thrive Global. Jaime has a BA in psychology from Boston University, a master's degree from New York University, and a certificate in Spiritual Psychology from the University of Santa Monica. Jaime's education and over twenty years of experience enable her to help her clients heal and see each challenge as an opportunity to evolve and grow. As an expert, Jaime is a trusted guide to manifesting love and to living a fulfilled life. Jaime's mission is to create a positive impact while changing lives worldwide.